# Breaking Free of OCD

## My Battle with Mental Pain and How God Rescued Me

### JEFF WELLS

LUCIDBOOKS

*For Gayle,*
*With Love*

# TABLE OF CONTENTS

# ACKNOWLEDGEMENTS

In the narrative, I mention some of the people whom God used to help me in this journey: Peter Johnson, Charlie and Rhonda Howell, Michael Mickan, Adam Cole, and, of course, my wife, Gayle. Certainly, our church family, WoodsEdge Community Church, has played a huge role, especially our elder team, our staff team, and my personal prayer team.

I owe deep gratitude to the encouragement and faithful intercession of John Lodwick, who remains, after 43 years, "a friend closer than a brother."

Glena Siebert, my assistant at WoodsEdge for nearly 20 years, has been a bigger help to me and partner in ministry than I could possibly express.

Also, I want to thank Sammantha Lengl from Lucid Books for overseeing this project. Laurie Waller further played an invaluable role in various editing processes. She made the book so much better!

# INTRODUCTION

## The Boston Marathon

In the 1978 Boston Marathon, I finished in second place to Bill Rodgers by two seconds. It was a thrilling race for me, and I felt overwhelmed with gratitude to God, not only for finishing second but also for running my personal best time of 2:10:15. I was humbled by God's grace and grateful beyond words.

But the thrill of second place at Boston had a shadow side, a secret known only to me. Deep down, I was relieved that I had not won. Let me be clear: I tried to win. I tried hard to win. I did my best. Yet, I was secretly relieved to finish second, not first. I did not dwell on it. I told no one. But I felt relief.

The 1978 Boston Marathon was run on a beautiful, cool day—the third Monday in April, as usual. There was a stellar field, including Bill Rodgers, the 1975 winner; Frank Shorter, the 1972 Olympic Gold Medalist and 1976 Olympic Silver Medalist; and many other top marathoners from around the world.

The weather was cool, so the leaders started out flying at well under a five-minute-mile pace. Although I didn't stay with the leaders at first, I still started out hard and in the hunt. The first 10 miles of the Boston Marathon are mostly downhill, but after the halfway point near Wellesley College, there is a series of five long, tough hills. The previous year had been extremely hot, and I had suffered terribly from the heat. On the last incline, Heartbreak Hill, I had edged into second place when

I passed Bill Rodgers at mile 20. But I was already extremely tired, with still six miles to go, and ended up having to walk some toward the end, finishing in twelfth place. It was a painful experience, both physically and emotionally.

Unlike the previous year, though, this time I ran strong going up the same difficult hills. I gradually began to move up in the field, and when I crested Heartbreak Hill, I had moved into sixth place. I was of course weary, but I still felt great. I had a lot of race left in me.

Could I catch the runners ahead of me? My body felt strong so I continued to give chase. I had only six miles to catch the leaders. In a few hundred yards, I edged into fifth place. In another half-mile or so I passed into fourth place. After a while, I passed Randy Thomas into third place. Then, with about two miles to go, I passed Essa Tikkanen of Finland to move into second place.

Now, only Bill Rodgers was ahead of me, and I was gradually gaining on him. Would I run out of course before I caught him? I was still several hundred yards back. During those last two miles of the race, I grew more and more fatigued, but I knew he was probably at least as tired. I was also exhilarated by the chase and the hope that I might catch him. With 300 yards to go, I pushed hard up the short hill on Hereford Street leading to the final stretch. Then I rounded the final turn about 20 yards behind Rodgers and gave it all I had to catch him in the last 120 yards.

But I came up just short. He finished two seconds ahead of me, the closest finish in the history of the Boston Marathon up to that point.

I was thrilled with my new best time of 2:10:15 for the 26.2 mile race. But here is the unusual part: I was secretly relieved that I had not won.

Let me tell you why. A few weeks before Boston, *Runner's*

*World* had run a story by Erich Segal, a Yale professor and the author of the novel *Love Story*. In the *Runner's World* story, a marathoner makes a Faustian bargain with the devil to win the Boston Marathon. A friend told me about the article, and the thought crept into my mind, "What if, in an irrational moment, I pray to Satan?" The thought began to torment and terrorize me. I obsessed over the fear that I might irrationally pray to Satan while trying to go over and over in my mind why I would never do that. I would confess my unbelief and worry to God, and gain some bit of relief. But relief was only temporary, and the tormenting thought would not go away for very long. The thought would come back again and again, thrashing me repeatedly. "What if I did that in a weak moment? That would be horrible, an unspeakable catastrophe! What if? What if? What if?"

The thought of committing such a horrible act plagued me. A normal person who had read that *Runner's World* article would have simply laughed at the notion and quickly dismissed it. But I was not normal. The fear of praying to Satan—even though that thought repulsed me—looped over and over again in my brain.

In the weeks before Boston, my biggest concern was not on the race itself, how prepared I was, or whom I would be racing. It was on this tormenting fear: "What if I prayed to Satan or made some kind of Faustian bargain in a weak moment? What if? What if?"

When the race finally came, I don't remember worrying about praying to Satan. I had enough to think about—the pace we were running, the race course, the next hill, the location of the top runners, the distance from the next water stop, how my legs were feeling. I was focused on the race itself. Moreover, in the last half of the race I was moving up in the field and was especially focused on catching each runner ahead of me.

I was thrilled to finish second and to run my best time by far of 2:10:15.

But when the race was over, I realized something. A part of me—a big part of me—was not just thankful, but relieved that I had finished second and not first at the 1978 Boston Marathon. Since I hadn't won, I would not have to wrestle with the thought that maybe, somehow, unwittingly, I had committed a Faustian bargain to finish first.

That's OCD.

## How It All Began

Let me go back two years before the marathon, when I first noticed that I had a problem. I was a senior in college at Rice University in Houston, Texas. My track team had made a trip to Philadelphia to compete in the Penn Relays and we were staying in a dormitory at the University of Pennsylvania. On our way out of the dorm, I grabbed an apple in the foyer to take with me. But later, after eating the apple, I began to have doubts: "Maybe I stole that apple. Maybe the apple was not meant for guests to take. Maybe this was a sin and will block my relationship with God and God's blessing in my life. Maybe God was displeased."

A more normal brain would have quickly dismissed this thought. After all, it was just an apple set out in the foyer, apparently for guests to take. But again, my brain was not normal. My overactive conscience flayed me, chewing me up and spitting me out. Over and over, I would rehearse the conflict of the University of Pennsylvania apple. Finally, after struggling for a week or so, I sent some money to university housing at Penn with an explanatory note. Whoever opened my letter probably couldn't believe it. Who would send money for an apple that had been set out for guests to eat? The person kindly sent me a commemorative Penn University ash tray (not much good for a marathoner!), and I was able to finally move on from the apple episode. That was the first episode of OCD that I can recall, but there were no doubt many smaller examples that I've successfully forgotten.

About a week later, I developed another problem. For many courses at Rice University, you could take the final on your own during a certain window of time. When I took my history final, a friend of mine had already completed it. Students at Rice take a strict honor code not to cheat or to help each other. My friend mentioned a few things about his final to me. He in no way was trying to cheat, but I immediately began to fret that he had said a little too much about the test. I obsessed that perhaps I had cheated on this final and that maybe my Rice graduation would be "tainted" in some way. Or, maybe I would not graduate at all.

I agonized over this problem for several days. I did not want to get my friend in trouble, but I felt compelled to do what was right. Finally, I went to the professor, Dr. Katherine Drew, the chairman of the history department. She had a rather serious countenance as I explained the whole situation to her, but then told me, "This is nothing. He did not say too much. Do not worry about it. Relax!"

Whew! I was relieved! Another problem averted. I was able to graduate from Rice University with a clean conscience.

Later that summer, though, after graduating from college and before going to seminary in the fall, I found myself struggling again with recurring thoughts and fears. For example, when I wrote letters (yes, we wrote letters, not emails, in the summer of 1976), I was hyperaware of honesty. If I dated the letter June 7th, but did not finish it until the next day, I felt compelled to indicate that I was now writing on the 8th. It was silly, trivial stuff, but it bothered me. If the speed limit said 55, then I needed to go exactly 55 and not 56. Even if the exit ramp seemed an unusually slow 20 miles per hour, I went exactly 20.

I became preoccupied with these trivial things, though they did not seem so trivial at the time. I worried about things that most people simply do not think twice about. During that summer between college and seminary, I slowly realized that something was wrong. "This can't be normal," I thought. "I must have some mental problem or condition. Most people don't struggle with the things I'm struggling with." A vague feeling of dread settled over me.

I didn't have a label or a term for this. I didn't know about obsessive-compulsive disorder. I didn't talk about this with anyone. But I was struggling inside. I was tormenting myself.

I suffered, and I suffered alone.

## Dallas Seminary

At the end of that difficult summer, I entered Dallas Theological Seminary in the fall of 1976. My roommate at Rice and my closest friend, John Lodwick, was also going to Dallas Seminary. We planned to room together at SMU graduate student housing and run with the SMU distance runners. I was excited about studying under storied professors at Dallas Seminary, such as Howard Hendricks and Charles Ryrie.

Unfortunately, my thought problems were getting worse, not better. For example, when taking a Greek test, I would worry that I might inadvertently see the paper of another student. So I kept my head down, eyes locked on my own paper. While that generally isn't a bad idea, I was overly nervous about seeing anything else.

Also, several professors would assign reading that we completed on an honor system. For example, in a given course we might be required to read 1,000 pages from a reading list. At the end of the semester, we would write and sign a little note, "On my honor, I have read 1,000 pages from the reading list."

That presented a big problem for me. Whereas most of the students were glad for the freedom, I agonized over every word. This was my thought: "If I say I read those pages, then I need to be sure that I read the entire page. Every word. And I need to make sure that I was paying attention to every word." So I began concentrating on whether I was concentrating rather than on what I was reading! Was my mind engaged on every word of that sentence? Was I fully concentrating? Could I honestly say that I had read that page? I reread so many sentences! I was paralyzed by my scrupulous conscience. It was ridiculous and exhausting, but I was seemingly helpless to approach the assignment logically. This went on for all four years of my seminary education.

The Boston Marathon of 1978 came in my second year of seminary. From that time on, I began to worry about upcoming races. What if I prayed to Satan instead of God in an irrational moment? This worry began to greatly complicate my running, which had been such a source of joy, gratitude, and freedom. I loved running. I ran for God because He had given me a gift, but now fear poisoned my running and robbed me of so much joy.

Other thoughts and fears tormented me, but this was the worst one: from time to time, I would wonder if I was even saved. Maybe I had not really trusted Christ as Savior on that beach in Galveston on July 4th, 1972. Perhaps I just thought I had. Maybe I did not have "real faith" or sufficient faith. What if I had not "done it right"? Now, this thought was terrorizing! What if I spent an eternity apart from God, apart from all my family and friends who knew the Lord, apart from all that was good, right, and joy-filled? What if I spent eternity in hell? Oh, the terror of this thought!

I would agonize and pray. I would go over verses in the Bible that promised salvation to all who believe.

But to all who did receive him, who believed in his name, he gave the right to become children of God (John 1:12).

For God so loved the world, that he gave his only Son, that whoever believes in him should not perish but have eternal life (John 3:16).

Truly, truly, I say to you, whoever hears my word and believes him who sent me has eternal life. He does not come into judgment, but has passed from death to life (John 5:24).

For by grace you have been saved through faith. And this is not your own doing; it is the gift of God, not a result of works, so that no one may boast (Ephesians 2:8-9).

I would go over and over verses like these and fret to myself: had I done this right? Had I really trusted Christ as Savior? Did I have genuine faith?

In my healthier moments, I knew I was a Christian. I knew that I was trusting Christ as my Savior and that He had saved me. I was fully surrendered to Christ, and I wanted to please God more than I wanted to breathe. But still . . . how could I be sure that I had really trusted Christ? What if I hadn't? What if? What if? This thought would torment me over, and over, and over. It felt like I was being pummeled and beaten to a pulp mentally—after a good thrashing I was left exhausted, defeated, and undone.

I did not talk much about my inward battle. I said little about it to my roommate, John, even though we were extremely close and lived together throughout college and even four years after college. I did not say anything to my parents, and, in fact, I did not talk with anyone about this problem. Instead, I suffered in silence, living inside my own head. I did not understand what was happening, but life was painful—more painful than the most excruciating marathon I had ever run.

One semester at seminary, I took a course in personality development, where I read for the first time about the perfectionistic personality. The author included a long list of traits that characterized the perfectionist, and I realized, "This is me. I am a perfectionist." I think he used the term *obsessive-compulsive personality*, but I couldn't find a lot of information about it. In the late 1970s, researchers didn't know a whole lot about obsessive-compulsive disorder, and it was seldom talked about.

During my seminary years, I finally gathered enough courage to talk to someone. I saw a couple of counselors, went once to a professor at Dallas Seminary who was a psychiatrist, and talked a couple of times to another Christian counselor in the city. They all cared. They were encouraging and hopeful, but I had no breakthrough or even improvement. My torment continued, and I had no idea of the challenges that I would have to face in the coming years.

## Oregon

In the spring of 1979, John Lodwick and I were invited by Nike to move to Eugene, Oregon for a year to train for the 1980 Olympics. At the time, Nike was a young, upstart company with its roots in distance running, and the University of Oregon at Eugene was the epicenter of distance running in the United States. We were excited to move there and train with top American runners trying to make the 1980 Olympic team. During that year, John and I would also serve as interns at a church in Eugene with a wonderful pastor, Mike Hilty.

On my very first Sunday in Eugene, I met a young woman, Gayle Shafer, at my intern church. A month later, Gayle and I began to date, and in the coming months we fell in love. The next February, on the Oregon coast, I asked her to marry me. (She told me, "I'll have to check my calendar!") Her fun-loving, prank-pulling, mischievous personality fascinated me. She was so refreshingly different than my over-serious, over-scrupulous, over-introspective personality.

My mental struggles continued during that year of training in Eugene—in fact, they got worse. I did not have tests and reading to worry about, but I still battled fears about running, fears about whether I was really saved, fears about committing some horrible sin. Sometimes, I even had the terrifying notion that I would hurt someone I loved, maybe stab them with a knife or something.

Moreover, I began to be preoccupied with certain numbers. I wore a simple Casio running watch (I still do). I was forever checking that watch, especially during runs when I was seeing how long I had been running or looking at my splits for intervals on the track. It seemed to me that certain numbers occurred too often, and that really bothered me. Specifically, 13, 23, and 31 bothered me. I don't know why these numbers affected me, but I basically felt, "These numbers occur too often. Something's wrong with that." Intellectually, I could reason my way out of this problem, but my thought problems weren't caused by a failure of logic. The source was deeper than that. Once I started noticing the numbers, I of course saw them all over the place. It was a bit like buying a car and then seeing that car everywhere. I was simply noticing what was already there.

Also, I began to be bothered by license plate numbers. I ran about 100 miles per week around the city of Eugene, and I would find myself checking license plates on the cars that drove by and feeling bothered by the patterns and numbers I saw. Again, it made no logical sense, but I felt that "something was wrong." I was harassing myself and was helpless to stop it. Life was so hard for me during this period, and I hated to be wasting so much valuable time on these ridiculous worries and fears.

Meanwhile, Gayle and I continued to date and were heading toward marriage. I had to tell Gayle about my thought problems, as embarrassing as I thought they were. Remember, I had basically hidden this problem from just about everyone, but these tormenting, scary thoughts that plagued me were a bizarre and significant part of my life. Normal people did not wrestle with things like this, and fully devoted followers of Jesus certainly did not. Especially pastors! So I kept it secret—but secrecy is just about always a bad thing.

However, I did not want to keep this a secret from Gayle any longer. It simply wouldn't have been fair to her to marry me without knowing the whole story, no holds barred. So, one day I summoned my courage and waded into it with her. I tried to describe the problem and how painful it was for me. Gayle listened patiently and lovingly, but how can a person without OCD understand the recurring thoughts that plagued me? "What if I pray to Satan? Am I really saved? What if I hurt a loved one? I am seeing too many 13s, 23s and 31s." (Who worries about this kind of stuff?)

I had not been sure how Gayle would respond, but she seemed unruffled and unshaken. She cared because she understood how painful it was for me, but she did not seem in the least deterred from marriage by my mental struggles. I was mostly relieved by her response, but at the same time I wondered if I had adequately conveyed the depth of my mental problem. If she really understood how bad this was, would she really want to marry me?

But at least she knew about it. I had brought this dark secret into the light, and she had not turned away from me. When I saw her response, I felt deeply accepted. I felt hope, hope that maybe I could survive this problem if the woman I loved walked with me and accepted me. About four months later, in June of 1980, we got married in Eugene, Oregon.

While I was right to talk with Gayle, I made a mistake in not talking more with John, who had been my roommate and closest friend for eight years. Since my OCD struggle had first surfaced during my senior year at Rice, I had largely battled it alone. This isolation was unhealthy, and I wish I would have talked about it with John freely and openly. I wish I would have blabbed about it until John was sick of it! John would have wanted to help me shoulder the burden, and certainly he would have been praying for me.

Occasionally, I would give John some idea of my struggle, but not much and not adequately. I never really spilled my guts about this huge problem in my life. I am not sure why I didn't, because I trusted John completely—I knew he was for me and would not reject me. Perhaps I did not think he could help, because he certainly did not struggle with this stuff. But mostly, I think I was too embarrassed. I felt guilty for the struggle and insecure because John was the godliest man I knew. Whatever the reason for my reticence, it was a mistake.

But no, I struggled alone, and it was a long and lonely journey. At times, I wondered if I might end up in an insane asylum of some kind. At times, I wondered if I would survive this. I was a tormented soul.

## Marriage

That summer during the Olympic trials in Eugene, Gayle and I were married and then moved to Dallas for my final year at Dallas Seminary. After our marriage, my OCD seemed to be as bad as ever, perhaps worse. In retrospect, I realize that my stress level was especially high with a new marriage, demanding graduate studies, rigorous marathon training, and racing in top-level marathons. I would later learn that stress exacerbates OCD, so it is no surprise that my OCD struggles were so difficult.

Sometimes, I was perfectionistic, picky, and rigid about things that did not matter. At other times, I was aloof and sullen. Gayle would naturally think, "He's mad at me. I must have done something wrong." But most of the time, I was simply battling some OCD fear in my head.

Maybe the thought would occur to me that I was not really saved, so I would have to go over and over in my mind why I was saved. I would review key Bible verses in my mind. I would pray; I would fret. I would go over and over the same things, my brain looping continually. No wonder Gayle felt that I was often preoccupied or upset with her. We struggled, and it was a tough first year of marriage.

I remember once during that year weeping in front of Gayle because of my mental anguish. This open breakdown was new for me—I didn't show much emotion in front of people. But at times, the pain simply overwhelmed me, leaving me bewildered, helpless, scared. At other times, the OCD struggle seemed to leave, but it would never go far. It was a daily battle, and in many ways, I was just trying to survive.

One year later, after I graduated from Dallas Theological Seminary, we returned to Eugene so I could be the college pastor at the church where we had met. I remember going a couple of times to a Christian counselor. He was kind and thoughtful, but this was the early 1980s and no one knew much about OCD in those days.

One conversation during this period still stands out to me.

I had lunch one day with Mike Hogan and Stu Barr, two men in our church. Mike was a federal magistrate, and Stu was a business owner. At some point during the lunch, I expressed some of the mental turmoil that I was experiencing. They were very busy men with full lives, but they insisted that we go to Mike's office so that we could talk and pray. Mike and Stu did not understand OCD. How could they? I had OCD, yet even I did not understand it! But they cared and hurt for me—I could see it in their eyes. Mike talked with me about the love of the Father, and Stu talked about the power of the Spirit. I shared with them, to some extent, my weakness and my weirdness, and they didn't reject me. Their compassion and love meant more to me than they knew—I was so encouraged. They were a model for me of the words of Paul in Romans 12:15: "Rejoice with those who rejoice, weep with those who weep." I will never forget Mike's and Stu's simple act of kindness. It was obvious that they cared.

At the time, I was still competing in marathons at a world class level yet continuing to struggle with the fear that in a weak moment I would pray to Satan. But during my training for the 1984 Olympic Trials, I developed chronic Achilles tendon pain, and though I attempted to run through it, I finally had to have surgery a few weeks before the Trials. Part of me was disappointed that I missed the Olympics, but much of me was relieved that I would not have the mental turmoil that came to me with running. To be clear, the turmoil was not the physical pain of running 26.2 miles at a fast pace. Instead, it was the silly fear, though so real to me, that I would pray to Satan in a weak moment. How I tormented myself!

This was not the only fear that bothered me. At times, the thought that I hadn't genuinely trusted Christ at my conversion would invade my mind. That fear might last a few days, or a few weeks, and then my mind would be on to something else, such as, "Is the Bible really true? Is Jesus really God?" The thoughts and fears would vary. I would obsess about one thing for a few days or a few weeks and then I would forget totally about it and begin to obsess about something else.

Other kinds of OCD could bother me. I am sure that I washed my hands more than the average person. I liked order in my personal space. But my OCD struggles were mostly in my mind. I later learned that my specific struggle was called scrupulosity. Over and over again, I had tormenting thoughts and fears that I would displease God in some terrible way.

The thoughts would wax and wane in severity but were never far away. I would surrender my fears to God, but they would always come back with a vengeance, wreaking havoc in my mind, filling my heart with fear, stealing all my joy.

Perhaps on the outside I appeared fairly normal to just about all the people around me. I served as a college pastor at a wonderful church in Eugene. I continued to train and run with Nike. I pursued my marriage with Gayle. Three years after we were married, we had our first child, a precious little girl named Sarah. But inside, in the place that only God and I saw, the mental anguish was unrelenting, and at times overwhelming.

## A Long Battle

In 1989, Gayle and I, along with our two small daughters, Sarah and Callie, moved to Houston, Texas to plant a church. We moved with high hopes and great excitement, but little did we know how arduous the journey would be.

Church planting was difficult—more difficult than we had expected. Two steps forward, one step backward. Finances were tough—both for our family and for the church. Inevitable conflicts surfaced between people, and some of our key members left. We tried a church merger that didn't work, forcing us to start all over again. Gayle and I sometimes fought because I tended to be preoccupied with getting the church started and with OCD thoughts. All in all, there was plenty of stress for us during this season, especially the first five or six years after we moved to Houston. However, several events occurred that helped alleviate my stress.

First, in 1993 Gayle and I had a breakthrough in our marriage. Because the church merger had not worked, I felt like a failure as a pastor. Gayle and I decided to see a wise, godly man, John Brickner, who soon discerned that our deepest issues stemmed from marriage instead of ministry. We spent the summer meeting with him, and these meetings helped enormously, helping me learn how to love Gayle better and make our marriage highest priority.

On one particularly difficult day in late 1993, I said to Gayle, "If you need me to stop being a pastor, I am willing to do that." She knew that I meant it, and my promise told her that she was more important to me than my ministry. Gayle had never really felt this before. She didn't want me to stop being a pastor—she just needed to know that she mattered more to me than our church.

Another encouraging event was that the church that we started in 1993, WoodsEdge Community Church, slowly began to pick up momentum and thrive. The financial pressure gradually began to subside as our church grew and became healthier. One additional change was that I quit competitive running. The 100th Boston Marathon in April of 1996 was my final competitive race.

But my struggles with OCD never went away. Over the next couple of decades, symptoms of OCD would come and go, but they would never go for long. I continued to struggle with all kinds of fears and doubts: Was it all true? Was Jesus really God? Was I really saved? Had I "done it right" when I trusted Christ as my Savior? I even struggled with doubts about leaving the church merger and starting over. Was this okay? Was it a horrible sin against God's church? How I agonized over this matter!

At some point, I even began struggling with the fear that maybe I would pray to Satan for someone to be healed. I would remind myself, over and over, why praying to Satan would be catastrophic and horrible, yet the fear that I would somehow slip still looped in my brain and tormented me.

Over the years, I tried to help my struggles in some way. I took medicine a couple of times, but only for a week or two and not nearly long enough to see results. I prayed a lot about the problem. At times, if it got bad enough, I would tell Gayle about my anguish. Sometimes, I would open the door of my mental pain and confide in someone else about my struggles. But even then, I would crack the door only slightly and never open it too widely.

I did not see a counselor for my OCD. I did not read widely on the problem to educate myself.

In retrospect, I did not really face this issue head-on. Whenever my problem with OCD got too bad, I would basically put a Band-Aid on it. I tried to avoid what I was thinking and not focus on it. But mostly, I just endured it, suffering inside more than anyone could know. Many times over the years, only God knew how painful this OCD became.

As the years progressed, however, and I continued to avoid fully confronting my symptoms, I would be moving toward a crisis in May of 2011 in which, at 57 years old, I would go through the darkest time of my life. Through this experience, God would put me in a position where I would be forced to confront all of the struggles I had endured over the years. This book is the result of everything that God taught me on my arduous journey. I trust that it will also be a help to you.

# THE NATURE OF OCD

# CHAPTER 1

## What Is OCD?

OCD is a complicated, difficult disorder that scientists understood little about even a few decades ago. However, we now know much more about the nature of OCD and can define both what makes up OCD and what causes it. Basically, people with this disorder have persistent unwanted thoughts (obsessions), and they attempt to deal with these unwanted thoughts with mental acts or repetitive behaviors (compulsions).

We can summarize obsessive-compulsive disorder with four succinct statements:

- OCD is a medical condition that is related to a biochemical imbalance in the brain.

- Obsessions are intrusive, unwanted thoughts and urges that do not go away.

- Compulsions are the repetitive behaviors that people perform in a vain attempt to rid themselves of the very uncomfortable feelings that the obsessions cause.

- Doing compulsions tends to make the obsessions worse, especially over the long run.

So this is the essence of OCD: chemicals and signals in the brain become confused and skewed, causing obsessions and compulsions. Obsessions are thoughts, emotions, and impulses that a person, to a great extent, cannot control, and compulsions are repetitive actions that a person acts out in order to cope with the overwhelming emotions and urges. Unfortunately, however, compulsions usually only worsen thought patterns, causing an unending cycle. In *The OCD Workbook*, Bruce M. Hyman and Cherry Pedrick explain that people with OCD "struggle with a neurobiological disorder that fills their minds with unwanted thoughts and threatens them with doom if they do not perform repetitive, senseless rituals."[1] They further explain, "OCD has many faces, but the style and manner of the thoughts and behaviors presented by people with the disorder are remarkably and unmistakably consistent."[2]

Some of the common obsessions include contamination obsessions, such as the preoccupation with avoiding dirt or germs; hoarding obsessions, so that you cannot throw away useless items; ordering obsessions, so that you have to order things "just so"; religious obsessions or scrupulosity, an excessive fear of having a blasphemous thought or sinful action; aggressive obsessions such as the fear of harming yourself or harming others or running over someone with a car; and sexual obsessions including fears of molesting your own children or other children. There are also various miscellaneous obsessions such as an excessive concern with certain numbers.

Common compulsions, which are the behaviors that OCD strugglers use to deal with these obsessions, include the following: cleaning and washing compulsions such as excessive hand washing or showering, checking compulsions such as checking locks or checking stoves or checking email, hoarding compulsions such as collecting useless items, ordering compulsions such as doing certain activities a prescribed number of times in the same order, and other miscellaneous compulsions.

Ian Osborn, both a follower of Jesus and a psychiatrist specializing in the study of obsessive-compulsive disorder, clarifies the four marks of clinical obsessions in order to clear up common misconceptions of OCD. He writes,

> Unfortunately, the terms *obsession* and *compulsion* are somewhat confusing. They have come to be used popularly in such a loose manner that their original psychiatric meanings have been all but lost. The term *obsession*, for instance, is often employed for what is more accurately termed a preoccupation, such as a coach's "obsession" with winning. *Compulsion*, on the other hand, is used to indicate anything done to excess, like compulsively eating sweets. The two terms put together, "obsessive-compulsive," commonly describe an individual who is unusually perfectionistic, time-conscious, and nervously driven to succeed. None of these meanings, astonishingly, has much to do with clinical OCD.

The unique and distinct nature of clinical obsessions was recognized early on. In the nineteenth century, when psychiatry was first emerging as a medical specialty, the German psychiatrist Karl Westphal provided an excellent definition that has not since been surpassed. Here's a simple version:

> Obsessions are thoughts which come to the foreground of consciousness in spite of and

contrary to the will of the patient, and which he is unable to suppress although he recognizes them as abnormal and not characteristic of himself.

The current, authoritative *Diagnostic and Statistical Manual of American Psychiatry* (DSM-IV-R; see appendix A) provides a more lengthy but similar definition. Both Westphal and the manual stress four important qualities that set apart the ideas, images, and urges that are clinical obsessions from other kinds of thoughts.

Obsessions, first of all, are *intrusive* thoughts. They pop into the mind abruptly, interrupting the normal flow. They are also *recurrent*. They keep on coming back again and again, in exactly the same form. Obsessions are *unwanted;* they are gate-crashers, intruders in the night, and as a result, a person fights to get rid of them. Here, the clinical meaning of the term stays close to its Latin root, *obsidere,* meaning to besiege, as an army would attack a city for the purpose of forcing surrender. Lastly, obsessions are recognized as *inappropriate.* Given a chance to sit back and reflect for a minute, the individual just can't figure out why the tormenting thought would ever have occurred in the first place.

Clinical compulsions, the other half of the equation, are purely secondary phenomena, acts performed solely to put right a tormenting thought. An obsession strikes, anxiety mounts, and a repetitive act provides a temporary way out. [3]

Jeffrey Schwartz, a medical researcher at UCLA and one of the top OCD authorities in the United States, relates one incident that Howard Hughes, a famous example of OCD, went through. It is encouraging to the person who struggles with OCD to see that even bright, gifted, highly successful people like Howard Hughes struggle with ridiculous things. I have never stayed in a bathroom washing my clothes for an hour and a half, but I have been plagued by scrupulosity and I have spent needless hours worrying about ridiculous things that many people don't worry about. OCD can't simply be willed away.

Howard Hughes was dining with actress Jane Greer at Ciro's on the Sunset Strip in Los Angeles one evening in 1947. At one point in the meal, he excused himself to go to the rest room. To Greer's amazement, he did not return for an hour and a half. When he finally reappeared, she was astonished to see that he was soaking wet from head to toe.

"What on earth happened to you?" she asked. "Well," Hughes said, "I spilled some catsup on my shirt and pants and had to wash them out in the sink." He then let them dry for a while, hanging them over one of the toilet stalls. Once he put his clothes back on, he explained, "I could not leave the bathroom because I could not touch the door handle. I had to wait for someone to come in."

According to Peter H. Brown, coauthor with Pat Broeske of *Howard Hughes: The Untold Story*, Jane Greer never went out with Hughes again.

Howard Hughes was eccentric, certainly, but he was not a freak. He was suffering from obsessive-compulsive disorder (OCD), a classic and severe case. By the end of his life, in 1976, he was overwhelmed by the disease. He spent his last days in isolation in his top-floor suite at the Princess Hotel in Acapulco, where he had sealed himself in a hospital-like atmosphere, terrified of germs. Blackout curtains at every window kept all sunlight out; the sun, he thought, might transmit the germs he so dreaded. Aides with facial tissues covering their hands brought him food, which had to be precisely cut and measured.

Rumors abounded that he was this reclusive because of drug abuse, a syphilitic condition, or terminal dementia. Actually, all his strange behaviors are readily understandable as symptoms of a severe case of OCD.[4]

This story saddens me because Hughes had to wrestle with this disease all of his life without any substantial help. We simply did not know that much when he was alive. It also saddens me because of my own story—I mourn all of the pain and wasted years of intense struggle. I know that God redeems those years and brings good out of them, but they were still extremely difficult, more difficult than I can express. I wish we would have known more in the spring of 1976 when I first became aware of my struggle.

The story of Howard Hughes also gives the person without OCD some glimmer into the nature of the disease. By all reports, Hughes was a brilliant man, but he could not think his way out of OCD, for ultimately the OCD struggle is not a matter of logic and reasoning. There are deeper issues involved.

# CHAPTER 2

# How Common Is OCD?

Medical professionals now understand that OCD is much more prevalent than once thought. Studies indicate that 2.5 percent of the US population, or 6.6 million people, suffer from obsessive-compulsive disorder—that is, one out of every 40 people.[1] This makes OCD the fourth most common psychiatric problem. However, just a few decades ago it was commonly thought by experts that there were far fewer cases of OCD. In his book, Dr. Ian Osborn talks about the common figure used when he was doing psychiatric training in the 1970s.

> When I was in training, the overall incidence of obsessive-compulsive disorder was thought to be extremely low. The figure most commonly quoted was a minuscule one-twentieth of one percent of the adult population. What was not appreciated, however, was how adept OCD sufferers are at keeping their disorder hidden. In 1983, when the National Institutes of Health announced the findings of the first large-scale study on the incidence

of mental health disorders in the U.S. population, the results took mental health professionals completely by surprise: OCD was found to occur in 1.9 to 3.3 percent of the population. The experts had been off by more than 4,000 percent in their estimate of the incidence of this disorder.

Yet even that oft-quoted figure is probably too low. The criteria used for the diagnosis of obsessive-compulsive disorder in the 1983 survey, called the Diagnostic Interview Schedule, were very strict. Individuals were said to suffer from OCD only if they had taken medication or sought a physician's help. More recent surveys that include all individuals who suffer significant distress as a result of obsessions and compulsions suggest a considerably higher incidence. A study from Zurich, Switzerland, for instance, concluded the 5.5 percent of people have suffered from such symptoms by age thirty.[2]

Dr. Osborn argues that probably five to ten percent of the population suffers from at least a mild case of obsessive-compulsive disorder at some point during their lives. That is an astounding figure, and it reveals that OCD is not a rare and unusual phenomenon. And, even if we use the more common figure of 2.5 percent of the U.S. population, that is still well over six million people in the United States alone.

At the church I now pastor, WoodsEdge Community Church, I have encountered numerous people who experience OCD. I've learned to mention my struggles with OCD and to elaborate on how bad those struggles have been over the years. I talk about my struggles with OCD because I want people to understand that our church is a safe place, that nobody has their act together, that all of us struggle, and that their pastor has struggled with mental disease. Because I talk about my own struggles with OCD, folks in our church who struggle with OCD have opened up to me. They also tell me about family members, usually children, who struggle with OCD. There are many of us at WoodsEdge who struggle with this problem, and that's just one church!

If no one around you seems to struggle with OCD, it may be that some people you know keep OCD a secret. Understand that you are not alone. Many people fight OCD every day, and there is so much help and support available that will give you hope and encouragement.

# CHAPTER 3
## Types of OCD

The first step to solving a problem is admitting to yourself that you have a problem. There are many people who struggle with OCD who know nothing about the disease and do not know that others struggle with the same things. Therefore, they are doing nothing to help solve the problem and get better.

Other people know a little about the disease but won't admit to themselves that they have it, refusing to attack the problem and get better. Both of these groups are missing out. Learning the different behaviors characteristic of OCD helps a great deal in identifying whether you suffer with it, and recognizing these symptoms in yourself can be the first step to healing.

Keep in mind that OCD is not monolithic. Everyone with OCD has clinical obsessions and clinical compulsions, but these obsessions and compulsions are expressed differently with different people, meaning that the symptoms will look a little different for each person. As you read the following primary types of OCD compiled by Hyman and Pedrick, be honest with yourself as to whether you struggle with these types of symptoms.

**Checkers** live with an excessive, irrational sense of being held responsible for possible dangers and catastrophes that may befall others as a result of their "imperfect" actions. They feel compelled to repeatedly check objects such as doors, locks, and the Off settings on household appliances to feel assured they've averted potential disasters they might have caused had they not checked. They might also check on loved ones to make sure they haven't caused harm to come to them. Checking relieves the anxiety brought on by the obsessive thought, but it is short-lived. The worries often return or are replaced by similar obsessive thoughts, calling for more checking. A cycle of anxiety, checking, limited relief, anxiety, and more checking is set up. Checking can be related to the obsessive fears or totally unrelated. For example, a man might check to make sure a door is locked after being struck by the fear that he had left the house without locking it. A student might check on a loved one after making a mistake on an assignment.

**Washers and cleaners** have obsessions about the possibility of contamination by dirt, germs, viruses, or foreign substances. They live with the near-constant dread of either causing or failing to prevent harm to others or to themselves by the actions of those agents of contamination. In response to their fears, they excessively wash their hands, shower, or clean their homes for hours on end. Over time, fears compound as they "detect" more possibilities for harm. The washing and cleaning become more and more elaborate, bringing less and less relief.

**Orderers and repeaters** feel they must arrange certain items in a particular, exact, "perfect" way, or they might repeat particular actions over and over. Many demand that particular objects, such as their shoelaces, hair, or personal belongings, be perfectly even or symmetrical. They become extremely distressed if their things are moved, touched, or rearranged even slightly. Obsessive thoughts or fears of harm coming to them or a loved one can lead to a frenzy of ordering or repeating certain behaviors over and over. They might cross over a room threshold repeatedly, count or repeat words silently, rearrange items, or turn light switches on and off until it feels "just right." Only then will the obsessive thoughts or fears subside, if only for a few moments.

**Pure obsessionals** experience unwanted, intrusive, horrific thoughts and images of causing danger or harm to others. The themes are almost always of a violent or sexual nature. Or they may have unwanted thoughts of acting upon a sexual impulse toward others in a manner that is clearly disgusting and repulsive to them. We call this type of OCD *pure obsessions* or "Pure-O," implying the presence of obsessive thoughts without accompanying *overtly* performed compulsions. Recent investigations of this type of OCD have revealed that most people with pure obsessions do indeed perform compulsions, but they are subtle, covert behaviors, such as mental compulsions or rituals. For example, many engage in repetitive thoughts, such as counting, praying, or repeating certain words, to counteract their anxious thoughts. They may also mentally review situations obsessively to ward off doubt and relieve anxiety. People with Pure-O may excessively monitor and scrutinize the feelings in their genitals for any "feelings" of arousal in unwanted circumstances. They often repeatedly ask others for reassurance that they are not going to harm someone. As with checkers, washers, orderers, and repeaters, these mental rituals bring temporary relief from the anxiety brought on by intrusive thoughts. With time, the relief lessens and mental rituals become more elaborate.

**Hoarders** collect insignificant items and have difficulty throwing away things that most people would consider "junk." They develop a strong attachment to their hoarded items and overvalue their importance. Often, they are afraid they might need the items at some vague time in the distant future. Letting go of things can cause so much distress that it is sometimes easier just to keep them.

**People with scrupulosity** obsess about religious, ethical, or moral issues. They demand a code of conduct from themselves that goes beyond that of others who subscribe to their beliefs. Their compulsions may involve prayer and seeking reassurance from others regarding their moral "purity." Rather than providing peace and freedom from the anxiety, compulsions bring limited relief, and the OCD demands more prayer, reassurance seeking, and other rituals.

Many people can identify with all these forms of OCD to some extent. Who hasn't checked to see whether the door is locked a second time? One person's prized, dusty old newspaper collection may be a pile of worthless junk to another. However, when behavior significantly interferes with daily living, OCD could be the problem.[1]

You may not fit neatly into any of these categories, but if you have clinical OCD, you have symptoms from at least one of these categories. For example, my basic struggle with OCD has been scrupulosity. My struggles have basically involved unwanted, indeed horrible, thoughts involving committing some great sin or displeasing God in some egregious way. But I also have some symptoms from the other categories. I do some checking, though my checking is mostly in the more modern form of checking my email. I like to keep my inbox clean! I wash my hands some, and I like neatness and order among my things, though this does not disrupt my life to a great extent.

But every person with OCD is different. Regardless of which symptoms you identify with, what all strugglers with OCD have in common is the biochemical imbalance that causes these painful obsessions and compulsions. Pay attention to your thoughts and actions, be truthful with yourself, and determine whether you think you struggle in some manner with OCD.

# CHAPTER 4

# Examples of Obsessions and Compulsions

Many people have some OCD tendencies, but that does not mean they all have full-blown OCD. Full-blown OCD has to be painful and significantly disruptive to your everyday life. In evaluating whether someone has OCD, we can look not only at the broad categories or types, such as what we saw in the previous chapter, but also at specific obsessions and compulsions.

Of course, no one with OCD will struggle with all of these symptoms, but if you have clinical OCD, you will struggle significantly with at least some of them. Keep in mind when reviewing this section that obsessions are the unwanted thoughts and urges that distress you. Compulsions are the senseless rituals you go through in a vain effort to get rid of these obsessions.

Here is a sample list from Hyman and Pedrick.

## Obsessions

### Contamination Obsessions

Excessive fear or disgust, and preoccupation with avoiding:

- bodily waste or secretions—urine, feces, saliva, blood
- dirt or germs
- sticky substances or residues
- household cleansing agents or chemicals
- environmental contaminants—radon, asbestos, radiation, toxic waste
- touching animals
- insects
- becoming ill from contamination
- making others ill by contaminating them
- diseases—AIDS, hepatitis, sexually transmitted diseases

### Hoarding, Saving, and Collecting Obsessions

- Worry about throwing things away, even seemingly useless items
- Urge to collect useless things
- Urge to pick up items from the ground
- Uncomfortable with empty space—feel need to fill it

### Ordering Obsessions

- Preoccupation with symmetry, exactness, or order
- Excessive concern that handwriting be perfect or "just so"
- Concern with aligning papers, books, and other items a certain "perfect" way

### Religious Obsessions, Scrupulosity

Excessive fear, worry, and preoccupation with:

- having blasphemous thoughts or saying bad things
- being punished for blasphemous thoughts
- concern with religious beliefs
- issues of right and wrong, morality
- dwelling on religious images or thoughts

### Somatic Obsessions

Excessive fear, worry, and preoccupation with:

- having an illness or negative reactions of others to one's appearance

### Aggressive Obsessions

Preoccupation and excessive, illogical fear of:

- harming yourself
- harming others
- acting on unwanted impulses—e.g., run someone over, stab someone
- harming others through your own carelessness

- responsibility for some terrible accident—or fire, burglary—especially if resulting from personal carelessness
- blurting out insults or obscenities
- doing something embarrassing or looking foolish
- violent or horrific images in your mind causing you to do harm to others

**Sexual Obsessions**

Unwanted, worrisome, and intrusive

- sexual thoughts, images, or impulses
- thoughts about molesting your own or other children
- thoughts about being or becoming a homosexual
- thoughts or images of violent sexual behavior toward others

**Miscellaneous Obsessions**

- Urge to know or remember certain things—slogans, license plate numbers, names, words, events of the past
- Fear of saying something wrong, not saying something just right, or leaving out details
- Worry about losing things
- Worry about making mistakes
- Easily bothered by certain sounds and noises— clocks ticking, loud noises, buzzing
- Easily bothered by the feel of clothing, textures on the skin

- Intrusive nonsense sounds, music, words
- Fear of saying certain words because of superstitious beliefs about particular words
- Fear of using certain colors for superstitious reasons
- Excessive superstitious fears with rigid adherence to them
- Excessive concern with lucky and unlucky numbers with rigid adherence to them

## Compulsions

### Cleaning and Washing Compulsions

Excessive, illogical, and uncontrollable

- hand washing, often performed in a ritualistic way
- showering or bathing, often performed in a ritualistic way
- ritualistic tooth brushing, grooming, shaving
- cleaning of the house, certain rooms, yard, sidewalk, car
- cleaning of objects, household items
- use of special cleansers or cleaning techniques
- avoidance of objects considered "contaminated"
- avoidance of specific places—cities, towns, buildings—considered "contaminated"
- concern with wearing gloves or other protection to avoid "contamination"

**Checking compulsions**

Checking over and over (despite repeated confirmation):

- that you did not harm others without knowing it
- that you did not harm yourself
- that others did not harm you
- that you did not make a mistake
- that nothing terrible happened
- that you did not do something that could cause future harm
- some aspect of physical condition, health—pulse, blood pressure, appearance
- physical surroundings—locks, windows, appliances, stoves
- that jars are closed by excessive tightening
- that doors are closed by excessive, repeated shutting, closing

**Hoarding, Saving, and Collecting Compulsions**

- Saving, collecting seemingly useless items
- Picking up useless items from the ground
- Difficulty throwing seemingly useless items away: "Someday I may make use of this . . ."

**Repeating, Counting, Ordering**

- Reading and rereading things, sometimes for hours
- Excessive worrying that you did not understand something you read
- Excessive writing and rewriting things

- Repeating routine activities—going in and out of doorways, repeated crossing of thresholds, getting up and down from a chair, combing hair, tying shoes, dressing and undressing over and over
- Doing certain activities a particular number of times
- Counting items—books on a shelf, ceiling tiles, cars going by
- Counting during compulsive activities, such as checking and washing
- Arranging items in a certain order—books, pencils, cupboards

**Miscellaneous Compulsions**

- Mental rituals—prayers, repeating "good" thoughts to counteract "bad" thoughts
- Reassuring self-talk or "mantras" stated over and over

  **Note:** These mental rituals are performed with the intention of reducing or neutralizing anxiety.

- Excessive need to repetitively ask others for reassurance when ample assurance is evident to others, and has already been provided by those around you
- Need to confess wrong behavior, even the slightest insignificant infractions of behavior toward others
- Superstitious behavior that takes excessive amounts of time
- Need to touch, tap, or rub certain items or people
- Measures, other than checking, to prevent harm to self or others—for example, avoidance of certain

objects or extreme precautions to prevent highly unlikely harm or danger

- Eating ritualistically according to specific "rules"—arranging food or utensils, eating at certain times, eating food in a particular order

**Related symptoms**

- Pulling own hair—from scalp, eyebrows, eyelashes, pubic area
- Acts of self-damage of self-mutilation—picking skin
- Compulsive shopping

   Note: Compulsive shopping is often related to hoarding—buying a number of things for fear of running out, for example.[1]

Again, so many people have at least some of these tendencies. That is not uncommon. But if you struggle very significantly with one or more of these symptoms, to such an extent that it is painful and disruptive of your life, you may well have OCD.

# CHAPTER 5

# Causes of OCD

Most of us who have struggled with obsessive-compulsive disorder have wondered, "What is wrong with me? Why am I thinking these thoughts? I must be such a sinful person!"

Similarly, family members and friends of those who have struggled with OCD have probably had similar thoughts at times: "What is wrong with him? Why doesn't he just snap out of it? If she really wanted to stop this behavior, she could. This is probably just a demonic attack."

We wonder, and our friends wonder, why all of this is happening. Remember, although there are of course other factors involved, the root cause of OCD is biochemical. Schwartz explains,

> In developing a new approach to treating people with OCD, our research team thought that if we could make patients understand that a biochemical imbalance in the brain was causing their intrusive urges, they might take a different look at their need to act on those urges and

strengthen their resolve to fight them. A new method of behavior therapy might result.

To help patients understand this chemical imbalance, we showed them pictures of their brains at work. During a study of brain energy activity in people with OCD, my colleague, Dr. Lew Baxter, and I took some high-tech pictures using positron emission tomography, or PET scanning, in which a very small amount of a chemically labeled glucoselike substance is injected into a person and traced in the brain. The resulting pictures clearly indicated that in people with OCD, the use of energy is consistently higher than is normal in the orbital cortex—the underside of the front of the brain. Thus, the orbital cortex is, in essence, working overtime, literally heating up.[1]

Elsewhere in his book, Dr. Schwartz reminds his patients to say, "It's not me, it's my OCD."[2] This is a great line for the person who struggles with OCD—brief, memorable, and powerful. You did not choose to have OCD. This is not who you really are. Remind yourself that this is not you—it is not reality. Rather, it's an OCD problem, ruled by biochemistry. The OCD struggler must understand this cause, and family members and friends of the OCD struggler must also understand this cause too.

Hyman and Pedrick elaborate even more about the cause of OCD. Medical studies continue to shed more light about chemical interactions within the brain of someone with OCD. It is, at its core, a biochemical problem, but genetic, environmental, and traumatic factors also contribute to the development of OCD.

No one knows exactly what causes OCD, but researchers are piecing together the puzzle. It appears that OCD results from a combination of genetically inherited tendencies or predispositions, combined with significant environmental factors. Inherited tendencies include subtle variations in brain structure, neurochemistry, and circuitry. Environmental factors include psychological and physical trauma, childhood neglect, abuse, family stress, illness, death, and divorce, plus major life transitions, such as adolescence, moving out, marriage, parenthood, and retirement. Inherited biological predispositions serve as a kind of tinderbox which, when combined with environmental lightning bolts, can ignite and activate OCD symptoms.

The most widely held biological theory of OCD is that it is related to abnormal functioning of one of the brain's vital chemical messengers—*serotonin*. Serotonin plays a role in many biological processes, including mood, aggression, impulse control, sleep, appetite, body temperature, and pain. Serotonin dysregulation has also been implicated in depression, eating disorders, self-mutilation, and schizophrenia (Yaryura-Tobias and Neziroglu 1997b).

Serotonin is one of the chemicals, called *neurotransmitters,* that nerve cells use to transmit energy impulses and to communicate with one another. Neurotransmitters do their work in the small space between two nerve cells, called the *synaptic cleft.* The transmission ends when the neurotransmitters are absorbed back up into the transmitting cell—a process that is called *reuptake.* Increasing the available serotonin through medication appears to produce changes in the *receptors* in some of the membranes of the nerves. It is believed that these receptors may be abnormal in people with OCD (Jenike 1996).

Brain-imaging studies have demonstrated abnormalities in several parts of the brains of people with OCD. These include the thalamus, caudate nucleus, orbital cortex, and cingulate gyrus. A study by Jenike and associates compared the brains of people with OCD with those of control subjects—people without OCD. Magnetic resonance imaging (MRI) showed a larger cortex (Jenike, Breiter, Baer, et al. 1996).

The *thalamus* processes sensory messages coming to the brain from the rest of the body. The *caudate nucleus* is part of the *basal ganglia,* deep in the center of the brain. The caudate nucleus controls the filtering of thoughts. Sensory information is sorted here. Normally, unnecessary information is disregarded. People with OCD become overwhelmed with intrusive thoughts and urges that the caudate nucleus does not filter out. The caudate of someone with OCD behaves like a doorman of an apartment building who does a poor job keeping out the undesirables.

The *orbital cortex* is in the front part of the brain, above the eyes. This is where thoughts and emotions combine. The caudate that is letting unnecessary thoughts and impulses through makes the job of the cortex much more difficult. The orbital cortex tells us when something is wrong and when we should avoid something. It is like an early warning system in the brain. It seems to work overtime in people with OCD.

The *cingulate gyrus* is in the center of the brain. It helps you shift attention from one thought or behavior to another. When it is overactive, we get stuck in certain behaviors, thoughts, or ideas. The cingulate is also the part of the brain that signals danger—that something horrible will happen if you do not carry out your compulsions.

Imagine all these parts of your brain screaming at you when your OCD symptoms are at their worst:

- The *thalamus* sends messages from other parts of the body, making you hyperaware of everything going on around you.

- The *caudate nucleus* opens the gate and lets in unwanted intrusive thoughts.

- The *orbital cortex* mixes thoughts with emotions, then tells you, "Something is wrong here! Take cover!"

- The *cingulate gyrus* tells you to perform compulsions to relieve the anxiety the rest of your brain has heaped on you.

- Meanwhile, your *synaptic clefts* are screaming, "Send in some more serotonin! We're running short here!"

By now you must be thinking: "No wonder I have problems!" Hopefully, you are also realizing OCD is not your fault. It is your brain! Of course we have simplified this greatly. Experts aren't even sure exactly what different parts of the brain do. As we said, the puzzle is still being pieced together.[3]

This excerpt from Hyman and Pedrick explains that, although the complexity of the brain makes understanding all aspects of OCD difficult, research has proven that biochemical reactions create OCD problems. But there are of course other factors that worsen OCD symptoms. My defective view of God and slowness to trust in Him might aggravate my struggles with scrupulosity. Also, I am quite sure that demonic attacks are at times involved. We know that we have a spiritual enemy, Satan and his hordes, who schemes against us. Certainly, stress and other physical factors can exacerbate OCD problems. However, we need to understand that the root cause of obsessive-compulsive disorder is biochemical.

Understanding this root cause does not excuse us from admitting that we have a problem and taking steps to deal with the problem in a healthy, God-pleasing manner. Just because the root issue is biochemical does not mean that I am helpless. Perhaps I need to take medicine, and certainly I need to pray and mobilize others to pray. I also might need to reduce stress in my life, and maybe I need to learn more about OCD and understand the nature of the problem.

Knowing the biochemical causes of OCD does not prevent us from admitting the problem and taking steps to deal with the problem. It does, however, help clarify the *nature* of the problem and help us get rid of misconceptions and false guilt. We cannot blame ourselves for struggling with OCD.

# CHAPTER 6

# Common Faulty Beliefs

One significant aspect of OCD is struggling with false beliefs. In other words, people who suffer with OCD often wrestle with lies that their minds tell them. Recognizing these faulty beliefs is essential in beginning to confront and conquer them. Also, these faulty beliefs can help someone determine that "Yes, I have OCD" or "No, I probably don't have OCD. That's not really the way I think."

Moreover, the following list from Hyman and Pedrick is a helpful resource for the person who struggles with OCD to sit down and talk with a trusted friend or family member: "This is what I struggle with at times." This might be a good conversation starter with a trusted friend. It can be very embarrassing for the person with OCD to talk about their struggles, because the emotions and thoughts can sound so ridiculous! Conversation starters are incredibly helpful in communicating what is going on in your mind. Obviously, the following list is not exhaustive, but it helps explain the types of faulty beliefs that those with OCD often battle.

1.  **Overestimating Risk, Harm, and Danger**

    - "I must protect myself (or others/loved ones) even if there is only the remotest chance of something bad happening. A tiny, one-in-a-million chance of something bad happening is exactly the same as a huge, 99.999 percent chance of something bad happening."

2.  **Black-and-White or All-or-Nothing Thinking**

    - "If I am not perfectly safe, then I am in great, overwhelming danger."

    - "If I do not do it perfectly, then I have done it horribly."

    - "If I do not perfectly protect others from harm, I'll be severely punished."

    - "If I do not perfectly understand everything I read, it is as if I do not understand anything."

3.  **Overcontrol and Perfectionism**

    - "I must maintain absolute control over my thoughts and actions, as well as control over all the circumstances that occur in my life. Unless I do everything perfectly, it is intolerable."

    - "Extreme harm and danger can come to me, my loved ones, or innocent others if I do not protect them perfectly."

    - "If it doesn't look or feel 'just right,' it is intolerable."

4. **Persistent Doubting**

   "Maybe I . . .

   - was not careful enough and therefore something bad will happen

   - harmed/molested/injured/cheated someone

   - stole/plagiarized/did something improper/immoral/bad

   - ". . . even though it makes no sense and doesn't agree with the facts."

5. **Crystal Ball or "What if?" Thinking**

   "In the future, what if I . . .

   - do it wrong?"

   - get AIDS?"

   - am responsible for injuring someone?"

6. **Magical Thinking**

   - "Thoughts are very powerful. Merely thinking a bad, horrible thought will certainly cause something horrible to happen."

7. **Superstitious Thinking**

   - "By doing my ritual (washing, tapping, repeating, touching, spinning, etc.), I can ward off bad things from happening to me and protect those I love."

   - "There are bad numbers and good numbers. Bad numbers cause bad things to happen and good numbers cause good things to happen or they can stop bad things from happening."

8. **Thought/Action Fusion (Similar to Magical Thinking)**

   - "If I have a bad, even a horrible thought about harming someone, it feels just as if I have actually done it."

   - "If I think about something bad happening, I am implicitly responsible should it actually happen."

9. **Overimportance of Thoughts**

   - "If I have a bad thought, it means I am bad, dangerous, or crazy."

   - "My thoughts are the true indicator of who I am, and what I am likely to do."

   - "I am judged as much by my thoughts as for what I actually do."

10. **Intolerance of Uncertainty**

   - "I must be 100 percent certain of everything, and I must be 100 percent sure that everything will be 'alright.' If I am the slightest bit uncertain about *anything* (my future, my health/loved ones' health), it is intolerable and I must do something, anything, to be certain that everything will be alright."

11. **Catastrophizing**

   - "An open sore on my arm means I'll *definitely* get AIDS if I am around someone I think has AIDS."

   - "If I get into arguments with my mother . . . it must mean I am *definitely* a violent person."

12. **Overresponsibility**

   - "Maybe I caused something bad to happen. My failure to prevent it must mean that I am certainly a bad person."

   - "I must always, at all times, guard against making a mistake that can possibly—even remotely—harm an innocent person."

13. **Extraordinary Cause and Effect**

   - "Objects have the ability to defy the forces of nature . . . for example, stoves can spontaneously turn on, refrigerators can open, locks can unlock—all without human intervention. Germs and viruses can leap long distances—even across city streets—and thus contaminate me and others."

14. **Pessimistic Bias**

   - "If something bad is going to happen, it is much more likely to happen to me or someone I love/care about than to others. This occurs for no other reason than it is me."

15. **Intolerance of Anxiety**

- "I can't stand being anxious for even a short period of time . . . I'll do anything to feel better now."[1]

People with OCD who have not seen such a list will probably think, "You mean, others struggle with that too? I'm not the only one who has this thought!" I struggle with some of these faulty beliefs and not at all with others. For example, I struggle with over-control and perfectionism, especially at the thought level. I want absolute control over my thoughts and feel guilty if a bad thought flitters through my mind. I can also struggle with persistent doubting: "What if that's not true? What if? What if?" Also, I have a basic intolerance of uncertainty—I want complete certainty when complete certainty is not available. On the other hand, I don't struggle at all with many of the points from the list. I don't really struggle with superstitious thinking or catastrophizing or pessimism. For the latter example, I tend to be a wild-eyed optimist in most things.

But knowing these faulty beliefs helps you identify the lies your mind tells you, bringing OCD out in the open and exposing it to the light. Martin Luther allegedly once made this helpful observation: "You cannot prevent a bird from flying over your head, but you can prevent the bird from building a nest in your hair." You may not ever get to the point of preventing a lie from entering your mind, but you can discipline yourself to confront the faulty belief when it appears. Knowing these faulty beliefs is an integral step on the road to healing.

(Hyman and Pedrick also suggest ways to challenge these faulty beliefs with self-talk. See their summaries on pages 104-105 of *The OCD Workbook*. Appendix 2 will give you specific information about the book.)

# HOW CAN I OVERCOME OCD?

What should I do if I have OCD? What are the foundational perspectives? What are some of the practical action steps?

Look at these as tools in your tool belt. Some of these tools you will want to use continually, making them part of your daily mindset. Some will be especially helpful to some people and less helpful to others. But all of these are valuable. Be aware of each tool and from time to time refer back to this list to make sure you are not forgetting something you need.

We will elaborate on this list in the following chapters:

1. Depend upon God

2. See yourself as God sees you

3. Soak in God's Word

4. Immerse yourself in God's love

5. Rest in the cross

6. Do not battle alone

7. Surrender

8. Commit to prayer

# CHAPTER 7

# Depend upon God

The first tool is to depend upon God and not yourself. Battling OCD is not a matter of trying on your own, but a matter of trusting God. We don't continue to struggle with OCD because we've never tried to fight it. Indeed, our problem might be that we are trying too hard and relying on our own efforts rather than relying upon God's power to transform us and rescue us.

There is an old couplet that I wrote in the front of my Bible as a young Christian:

When I try, I fail.
When I trust, He succeeds.

I should have written this couplet on my heart, not just in my Bible. The words don't mean that we stop working toward healing, but that we fundamentally trust in God and not in our own efforts.

This charge to depend upon God and not ourselves is God's message to us throughout the Bible. It is God's message to us in Genesis 15 when Abraham believes God and is justified, or made right with God, by his faith alone. This same message, to depend upon God and not ourselves, is taught throughout the lives of the patriarchs—Abraham, Isaac, Jacob, and Joseph—as God teaches them to rely upon Him and not on themselves.

It is the identical message that God taught His people throughout the Old Testament: people like Moses and Joshua, David and Daniel, Isaiah and Jeremiah. It is also the message that we see in the Gospels as Jesus repeatedly rebukes His disciples for their failure to trust Him, and He commends those people who do trust Him. For example, when the Roman centurion trusts Jesus' healing power, Jesus responds, "With no one in Israel have I found such faith" (Matt. 8:10).

We also see Paul calling us to live by faith. For example, in Romans 14:23 Paul charges us, "Whatever does not proceed from faith is sin." And then in the great Hall of Faith chapter, Hebrews 11, time after time we see that men and women of God have always lived by faith. God's message throughout the Bible is emphatic and repeated: "Trust me! Depend on me and not yourself. I love it when you dare to live by faith."

Whenever we trust God and depend upon His power, the Holy Spirit unleashes His power. The Christian life is a supernatural life and must have supernatural power—the power of the Holy Spirit.

Hear God's call to you:

Not by might, nor by power, but by my *Spirit*, says the Lord of hosts (Zech. 4:6).

*Trust* in the Lord with all your heart, and do not lean on your own understanding. In all your ways acknowledge him, and he will make straight your paths (Prov. 3:5-6).

Do not let your hearts be troubled. *Trust* in God; *trust* also in me (John 14:1 NIV).

And without *faith* it is impossible to please him, for whoever would draw near to God must *believe* that he exists and that he rewards those who seek him (Heb. 11:6).

If you are struggling with mental disease, understand that the power to change is *in* you but not *from* you—the power is *from* the Holy Spirit. Depend upon the Lord, depend upon the Spirit, depend upon the power of the Spirit.

When it comes to OCD or mental disease, or any other challenge of life, the solution is not to try harder with your own strength. The solution is to depend upon God's power to transform you. When it comes to OCD, do not grit your teeth and repeat to yourself with steely determination, "I can stop this behavior. I can beat this thing. I can conquer these fears." Rather, say to God, "Lord, I cannot change. Lord, I do not have the power to conquer this. Lord, would you give me grace to conquer it? I depend upon the resurrected power of the risen Christ, the power of the Holy Spirit!"

Write this truth on your heart:

When I try, I fail.
When I trust, He succeeds.

*O Lord, give us grace to trust You. May we depend, deeply, on You, on Your strength, on Your power. Amen.*

# CHAPTER 8

# See Yourself as God Sees You

The second tool in overcoming mental disease is to see yourself as God sees you. At one point on my journey to freedom, I realized that I still saw myself as an addict—an OCD addict. I felt God nudging me: "That's not who you really are. That's not the essence of who you are. Don't see yourself that way. Give that up."

Since the age of 21, I had struggled with OCD in all kinds of areas, and at some point along the way, I had begun identifying with OCD. A person with OCD—that was who I was. But in the last few years, I have realized more and more that this struggle with OCD does not define me and cannot define me. It is not the essence of who I am.

What is my essential identity? I am a child of God. That is the heart of my identity—a much-loved, blood-bought child of God. God's adopted son, fully accepted, fully loved, fully forgiven, safe in Christ.

What difference does it make how I see myself? Or how you see yourself? In every way, it matters. How you see yourself matters.

The most important belief for any of us is how we see God. But the second most important thing is how we see ourselves. For example, take the man who has struggled a long time with pornography. He tends to think of himself, in regard to women, as a predator.

But what if he realized that, because he is in Christ, he is not in essence a *predator* of women, but a *protector* of women? Deep down, this is his true heart's desire—not to abuse women and view them as sexual objects, but to protect women and view them as precious daughters of God. If he began to see himself this way, to really see himself this way, would this make a difference? When he saw a woman dressed seductively, then he would feel protective of her, not predatory toward her. "Oh, Lord, protect her. Draw her to You. Help her to realize that all she really needs is found in You, not in men or the approval of others."

Identity matters. That is why the New Testament is chock full of truths on who we are in Christ. And that is also why Satan feeds us lies, deceptions, and accusations about who we are.

God also used an image from the movie *The Shawshank Redemption* to help shape my understanding of how He sees me. When Adam Cole, my close friend, told me about this picture of institutionalized prisoners, a picture that Adam felt God had given him for me, it immediately rang true in my life. In the movie, so many of the prisoners could not live outside the prison walls—in some ways they were slaves to their prison cells. "This is where I belong. This is where I have comfort— even if it is a twisted comfort." But this was not true of Tim Robbins' character, Andy Dufresne. He knew he could live on the outside, that he did not belong in the prison, that prison was not his identity. Rather, he belonged on a beach in Cabo, living as a free man.

Adam raised questions for me: Did this image resonate with me? Had I come to see myself as belonging to the prison cell of OCD? Did I derive a comfort, even a twisted comfort, from the familiar torments of OCD?

And I had to admit to myself that this image did fit me. Unfortunately, I had come to see myself as belonging to the prison cell of OCD torment. But it was not true! It was a lie. Yes, I struggled with OCD, but I was not a slave to OCD. I did not have to live in Shawshank—I could live in Cabo. *That* is my identity.

Friend, see yourself as God sees you. This is the truth about who you are, and the truth will set you free.

There is much more to say about how God sees you—more than I can say here. But these verses are a great start.

**You are a child of God.**

John 1:12: "But to all who did receive him, who believed in his name, he gave the right to become children of God."

1 John 3:1a: "See what kind of love the Father has given to us, that we should be called children of God; and so we are."

**You are much loved by the Father.**

Romans 5:8: "But God shows his love for us in that while we were still sinners, Christ died for us."

1 John 4:10: "In this is love, not that we have loved God but that he loved us and sent his Son to be the propitiation for our sins."

**You are an adopted child of God.**

Romans 8:15: "For you did not receive the spirit of slavery to fall back into fear, but you have received the Spirit of adoption as sons, by whom we cry, 'Abba! Father!'"

Galatians 4:4-5: But when the fullness of time had come, God sent forth his Son, born of woman, born under the law, to redeem those who were under the law, so that we might receive adoption as sons."

**You are free in Christ. You are not a slave.**

Galatians 5:1: "For freedom Christ has set us free; stand firm therefore, and do not submit again to a yoke of slavery."

John 8:32: "And you will know the truth, and the truth will set you free."

**You are righteous—right with God—because of Jesus.**

Romans 5:1: "Therefore, since we have been justified by faith, we have peace with God through our Lord Jesus Christ."

Romans 4:5: "And to the one who does not work but believes in him who justifies the ungodly, his faith is counted as righteousness."

**You are completely forgiven of all your sin.**

Colossians 2:13-14: "And you, who were dead in your trespasses and the uncircumcision of your flesh, God made alive together with him, having forgiven us all our trespasses, by canceling the record of debt that stood against us with its legal demands. This he set aside, nailing it to the cross."

Psalm 103:12: "As far as the east is from the west, so far does he remove our transgressions from us."

**You are dead to sin but alive to God in Christ.**

Romans 6:11: "So you also must consider yourselves dead to sin and alive to God in Christ Jesus."

**You have a sound mind.**

2 Timothy 1:7: "For God gave us a spirit not of fear but of power and love and self-control."

**You are under no condemnation because of sin.**

Romans 8:1: "There is therefore now no condemnation for those who are in Christ Jesus."

**You are holy, a saint.**

Romans 1:7: "To all those in Rome who are loved by God and called to be saints: Grace to you and peace from God our Father and the Lord Jesus Christ."

1 Peter 2:9-10: "But you are a chosen race, a royal priesthood, a holy nation, a people for his own possession, that you may proclaim the excellencies of him who called you out of darkness into his marvelous light. Once you were not a people, but now you are God's people; once you had not received mercy, but now you have received mercy."

(The root word in Greek for *saints* is the same as the Greek word for *holy*. When God says we are saints, He is telling us we are holy ones, or holy in Christ. We are a holy people.)

**You are safe and secure forever in Christ.**

Romans 8:38-39: "For I am sure that neither death nor life, nor angels nor rulers, nor things present nor things to come, nor powers, nor height nor depth, nor anything else in all creation, will be able to separate us from the love of God in Christ Jesus our Lord."

John 10:28-29: "I give them eternal life, and they will never perish, and no one will snatch them out of my hand. My Father, who has given them to me, is greater than all, and no one is able to snatch them out of the Father's hand."

Christian, let these truths sink in: you are a child of God. You are much loved by the Father. You are an adopted child of God. You are free in Christ. You are not a slave. You are righteous, right with God, because of Jesus. You are completely forgiven of all your sin. You are dead to sin but alive to God in Christ. You have a sound mind. You are under no condemnation because of sin. You are holy, a saint. You are safe and secure forever in Christ. *This* is who you are. This is who *you* are. This is who you *are*.

Your identity does not rely on what you have done, but on what Christ has done. Will you see yourself as Satan sees you, or will you see yourself as God sees you? Will you live in the lies of the evil one who is bent on destroying you, or will you live in the truth of God's Word? Will you live in the Shawshank prison of bondage and lies, or will you live in the freedom of Cabo?

What about it? It is your choice.

Christian, let's go with the truth of God and God's Word! For His glory! And for our joy!

*Lord, give us grace. Give us grace to see ourselves the way You see us, the way we really are. Lord, do this for Christ's sake, we pray. Amen.*

# CHAPTER 9

# Soak in God's Word

The third tool is to soak in the truth of God's Word.

The Word of God is alive. It is powerful. It is soul-transforming. The writer in Hebrews reveals the penetrating power of Scripture: "For the word of God is living and active, sharper than any two-edged sword, piercing to the division of soul and of spirit, of joints and of marrow, and discerning the thoughts and intentions of the heart" (Heb. 4:12).

The truth of God's Word sets people free. Jesus said in John 8:32, "And you will know the truth, and the truth will set you free." And where do we go to find this truth that sets us free? We go to God's Word. In John 17:17, Jesus declares in His prayer to the Father: "Your word is truth." So as we immerse ourselves in God's Word, as we soak in God's Word, we are set free by the truth of the Word of God.

If you struggle with OCD, then you must meditate on God's Word and soak in God's Word. You must fill your mind with God's Word because in God's Word there is truth—life-liberating truth. There is life. There is power. There is hope. There is freedom. This is of course true for all people, but it is especially true for those who struggle with OCD.

It is no surprise that Jesus constantly referred to the Scriptures, over and over again. Moreover, every time Jesus referred to the Bible, He did so with complete confidence in the authority and veracity of Scripture. For example, in Matthew 4, three times Satan comes at Jesus with temptation, and three times Jesus responds by quoting Scripture. "It is written. It is written. It is written!" For Jesus, if it was found in Scripture, that settled things.

Jesus not only quoted Scripture, but He also *obeyed* Scripture. He submitted to Scripture. He was not just a hearer of God's Word—He was a doer of God's Word.

Claim any Scripture that speaks to any aspect of the battle with mental disease. You might make a list of those verses that you find especially helpful. Go over them. Learn them. Meditate on them. Let them percolate in your soul. Here are some verses that have helped me with the struggles that I have had with mental disease:

1.  Proverbs 3:5-6: "Trust in the Lord with all your heart and do not lean on your own understanding. in all your ways acknowledge him, and he will make straight your paths."

    *Remind yourself over and over again: Trust the Lord. Trust the Lord. Lean not on your own understanding.*

2.  John 14:1: "Do not let your hearts be troubled. Trust in God; trust also in me" (NIV).

    *Perhaps I have gone over this verse more than any other verse. We do not have to be troubled. It is a choice we can make: "Let not your heart be troubled."*

3. Philippians 4:6-7: "Do not be anxious about anything, but in everything by prayer and supplication with thanksgiving let your requests be made known to God. And the peace of God, which surpasses all understanding, will guard your hearts and your minds in Christ Jesus."

*A great promise to marinate in, with specific, practical commands, including the exhortation to not simply make a request but to give thanks as you are making your request.*

4. 1 Corinthians 10:13: "No temptation has overtaken you that is not common to man. God is faithful, and he will not let you be tempted beyond your ability, but with the temptation he will also provide the way of escape, that you may be able to endure it."

*Yes, we are tempted. But our temptations are not unique. Others have been tempted in this way. We do not have to succumb. God will give us the power to say "No."*

5. Psalm 55:22: "Cast your burden on the Lord, and he will sustain you; he will never permit the righteous to be moved."

*Take your burden and bring it to God. Cast it upon Him and do not carry it yourself.*

6. Matthew 11:28: "Come to me, all who labor and are heavy laden, and I will give you rest."

*Come to Jesus. Come to Jesus and leave your burdens with Him. He is an unending source of rest and peace.*

7. John 16:33: "I have said these things to you, that in me you may have peace. In the world you will have tribulation. But take heart; I have overcome the world."

   *Yes, this world is tough. There is tribulation and trial. But display courage! Christ has overcome the world.*

8. Matthew 28:20: "Teaching them to observe all that I have commanded you. And behold, I am with you always, to the end of the age."

   *No matter what, Christ will be with us. He will be right there, beside us, before us, behind us, beneath us, above us, with us, for us, in us. Every step of the way.*

9. Hebrews 13:5: "I will never leave you nor forsake you."

   *No matter how we struggle, how we fail, how confused we might be, Christ will not leave us. Ever.*

10. 2 Timothy 1:7: "For God gave us a spirit not of fear but of power and love and self-control."

    *God has not given us a spirit of fear. He has given us power and love and a sound mind. We can say "No" to fear. We do not have to be slaves to fear.*

These are just ten of the verses that have meant so much to me. Add to these verses—make your own list. Soak in them. Live in them. Revel in them.

*Lord, thank You for Your holy Word. Would You fill our minds with Your mind? Lord, help us to hide Your Word in our hearts. Transform our minds, our hearts, our souls. For Your glory. Amen!*

# CHAPTER 10

# Immerse Yourself in God's Love

A fourth tool for overcoming OCD is to immerse yourself in God's love.

A.W. Tozer, in his superb little book *The Knowledge of the Holy* (which I count as my all-time favorite book), begins with this stirring thought: "What comes into our minds when we think about God is the most important thing about us."[1] Tozer's incisive comment is especially true of God's love: "What comes into our minds when we think about *God's love* is the most important thing about us." Even more specifically, "What comes into our minds when we think about God's love *for us* is the most important thing about us."

During the period of my life when I was serving as a young pastor, I realized that my view of God was defective—I did not *feel* loved by God. I *felt* that God was sovereign, great, holy, and powerful. But, if I was honest with myself, I did not really *feel*, deep inside, that God was kind, gentle, loving, and forgiving.

I preached that God was loving and kind. I said that God was loving and kind. I talked about God being loving and kind. But at some level, deep inside, I *felt* that God was a stern taskmaster, and hard to live with.

It was a painful realization to admit to myself that deep down I struggled to believe in God's tender love for me. But God in His mercy pulled back the curtains of my soul and gave me a glimpse at my unbelief in His goodness.

How did this faulty view of God's love and tenderness affect my struggles with obsessive-compulsive disorder? I was not sure then, and I am not completely sure today. I do not think that this misconception about God caused my OCD. The OCD was rooted in brain biochemistry and exacerbated by a number of factors—including unbelief in God's love and mercy. However, I imagine that my faulty view of God fed my OCD problems and that my OCD problems fed my faulty view of God.

When I realized that I did not feel loved by God, I knew that I had to do something, because this belief was crucial to my relationship with God. It affected everything. For example, without feeling loved by God, I would not love God back. I might have religious duty, but I would not have a love affair with God, and Jesus is quite clear in the Gospels that loving God is the most important of all the commandments (Matt. 22:34-40).

Moreover, if I did not feel deeply loved by God, then I would not trust God—at least not for the hard stuff. I mean, could I really trust God for the tough things of life if I did not feel tenderly loved by Him, if I looked at Him as a harsh taskmaster? Doubtful.

Indeed, if I did not feel tenderly loved by God, I would not fully love Him, trust Him, obey Him, enjoy Him, worship Him, or seek Him. Sensing that you are loved by God is the entire foundation for the spiritual life! No wonder Paul prays that believers at Ephesus would be "rooted and grounded in love" and that they would "comprehend with all the saints what is the breadth and length and height and depth, and . . . know the love of Christ that surpasses knowledge" (Eph. 3:17-19).

Knowing God's love, for me, was paramount. Not knowing it with my head, but knowing it with my heart and with the deepest fibers of my soul.

So, when I realized that I struggled with the love of God, I set out on a journey, a journey to better grasp God's love for me. I sensed that the stakes were high, that this belief was critical to my spiritual life, and perhaps critical to my mental anguish.

I began to change. First, I prayed. Desperately. *"Oh, God, help me to see You as You really are! Help me to grasp how much You love me!"* When I came across a verse or a passage that explained God's mercy, kindness, and love, my antenna would go up and I would be especially alert to what the Bible said.

Moreover, I read books that helped me to realize God's love and kindness. I remember reading one of A.W. Tozer's books that included this line: "God is easy to live with."[2] That jarred me. "God is easy to live with!" I knew it was true. But I did not *feel* that truth inside. I certainly did not live as if God were easy to live with.

In addition to desperate prayer, intentional Bible reading, and reading Christian books, God also used worship in my life, especially corporate worship. We had a gifted worship leader in our church in Oregon whose guidance helped me experience the power of worship. When you connect with God in worship, when you express your love and adoration to your God, when you sense His presence and personally sing to Him, something powerful happens in your soul: your image of God is transformed. I think God used worship to slowly transform the way I saw Him.

Let me be clear: With this desperate quest to feel God's love,

I did not experience an immediate change—a light switch did not flip on in an instant. But I realized that I had a problem and that I could face it. It is hard to work on a problem if you deny that you have one.

Change didn't happen overnight, but slowly, over years, decades, I began to see God differently. Thirty years later, I am still on that journey. I am not where I want to be, but at some point I realized that my view of God had changed, that I was beginning to feel loved by God, tenderly loved by God. I began to feel that God is in fact easy to live with. I am not where I used to be.

Again, I have a long way to go, but today I enjoy God's love so much more freely. Knowing that I am tenderly loved by God has been crucial to every part of my life and has been foundational to my healing of mental anguish.

If we believe in our heart of hearts that the God of the universe has an overwhelming love for us, this belief will change everything in our lives. If we know—not just with our minds, but with our hearts—that God is crazy in love with us, this knowledge will transform our life. If we understand that God's love for us is personal, tender, and unchanging, this understanding will bring about so many changes—we will love Him back, we will trust Him, we will obey Him, we will enjoy Him, we will enjoy life, we will rest in Him, we will worship Him. God's love for us is the foundation for all of life.

Yet, most of us can be so slow to believe in God's love for us. One reason that we can be slow to believe in God's love for us is that life can be so difficult, filled with pain and suffering, and we often tend to blame God. Also, there is our own sinful unbelief in God's goodness and love, which is part of the original sin that we are all born with. Satan's main strategy in attacking us is to get us to doubt God's love for each of us, individually. We see this the very first time Satan appears in the biblical record in Genesis 3, when he suggests to Eve that God isn't really good and loving and therefore cannot be trusted. A.W. Tozer wrote that "Satan's first attack upon the human race was his sly effort to destroy Eve's confidence in the kindness of God . . . Nothing twists and deforms the soul more than a low or unworthy conception of God."[3] For all of these reasons, and more, we struggle to believe that the God who made us loves us with a relentless, tender affection.

Martin Luther once stated, "This is that ineffable and infinite mercy of God which the slender capacity of man's heart cannot comprehend and much less utter—that unfathomable depth and burning zeal of God's love toward us."[4] G.K. Chesterton remarked, "All men matter. You matter. I matter. It is the hardest thing in theology to believe."[5]

So, on one hand, God's love for us is the most important thing in theology, and on the other hand, it is the most difficult thing in theology. On one hand, God's love for us is so vital, and on the other hand, it is so elusive. If God's love is a struggle for nearly all Christians, this is especially true for Christians who battle obsessive-compulsive disorder. Most of us who battle OCD also struggle with believing and enjoying God's tender love for us.

To face this challenge, this is what I now do: every morning, first thing, I immerse myself in the love and grace of God. I receive God's love. I bask in His love. I let God love me. I express my responsive love back to God: "I love You, Papa. I love You, Jesus. I love You, Spirit." I receive His love for me. I feel His love for me. I let God love me. I sing to Him, perhaps with a song on my iPhone or iPad.

In the notes section of my iPad, I go over some of my favorite verses on God's love and grace. This list of verses on my iPad includes the following:

Exodus 34:6-7: The Lord passed before him and proclaimed, "The Lord, the Lord, a God merciful and gracious, slow to anger, and abounding in steadfast love and faithfulness, keeping steadfast love for thousands, forgiving iniquity and transgression and sin, but who will by no means clear the guilty, visiting the iniquity of the fathers on the children and the children's children, to the third and the fourth generation."

Psalm 86:15: "But you, O Lord, are a God merciful and gracious, slow to anger and abounding in steadfast love and faithfulness."

Psalm 103:8: "The Lord is compassionate and gracious, slow to anger and abounding in steadfast love."

Psalm 103:11: "For as high as the heavens are above the earth, so great is his steadfast love toward those who fear him."

Psalm 103:12: "As far as the east is from the west, so far does he remove our transgressions from us."

Jeremiah 31:3: "I have loved you with an everlasting love."

Romans 5:8: "But God shows his love for us in that while we were still sinners, Christ died for us."

Romans 6:11: "So you also must consider yourselves dead to sin and alive to God in Christ Jesus."

Romans 8:1: "There is therefore now no condemnation for those who are in Christ Jesus."

Romans 8:15: "For you did not receive the spirit of slavery to fall back into fear, but you have received the Spirit of adoption as sons, by whom we cry, 'Abba! Father!'"

Galatians 2:20: "I have been crucified with Christ. It is no longer I who live, but Christ who lives in me. And the life I now live in the flesh I live by faith in the Son of God, who loved me and gave himself for me."

Galatians 5:1: "For freedom Christ has set us free; stand firm therefore, and do not submit again to a yoke of slavery."

Colossians 1:13-14: "He has delivered us from the domain of darkness and transferred us to the kingdom of his beloved Son, in whom we have redemption, the forgiveness of sins."

Colossians 2:13-14: "And you, who were dead in your trespasses and the uncircumcision of your flesh, God made alive together with him, having forgiven us all our trespasses, by canceling the record of debt that stood against us with its legal demands. This he set aside, nailing it to the cross."

2 Timothy 1:7: "For God gave us not a spirit of fear but of power and love and self-control."

1 John 3:1: "See what kind of love the Father has given to us, that we should be called children of God; and so we are."

1 John 4:10: "In this is love, not that we have loved God but that he loved us and sent his Son to be the propitiation for our sins."

1 John 4:18: "There is no fear in love, but perfect love casts out fear. For fear has to do with punishment, and whoever fears has not been perfected in love."

Revelation 1:5-6: "To him who loves us and has freed us from our sins by his blood and made us a kingdom, priests to his God and Father, to him be glory and dominion forever and ever. Amen."

Usually, I will choose and ponder one of these verses every day. I soak in it. I remind myself of the truths of God in order to counter the lies of Satan or the unbelief in my own heart. I want to brainwash my mind with God's truth so that I can be transformed by the renewing of my mind. Many other verses can also provide great help, but these are the ones on my list so that I can daily remind myself that I am completely forgiven and forever loved. I am a much-loved, blood-bought child of the living God.

This is not a short-term solution to OCD struggles. This is long-term. But this is foundational, and the foundation, for anything, is the most important thing. The more I soak in God's love and grace, God's compassion and mercy, God's relentless affection and tender kindness, the less susceptible I am to OCD fears and struggles. Indeed, the more I soak in God's love and grace, the better every area of my life functions.

*O Lord, show us Your love. Show us Your grace. May we be rooted and grounded in love. May we know how long and wide and high and deep Your is love for us. May we know, deeply and personally, this love, a love that surpasses understanding. Amen.*

# CHAPTER 11

# Rest in the Cross

The fifth tool is to rest in the cross of Christ.

This is the center of biblical faith—the cross of Jesus Christ. The main reason Jesus came to the planet was to die on the cross, and the primary proof of the Father's love for us is the cross. The Old Testament points forward to the cross, and the New Testament looks back to the cross. If we fail to grasp the cross, to focus on the cross, to live in light of the cross, then our faith is less than fully biblical. Biblical faith is Christ-centered and, more specifically, cross-centered.

If we grasp that Jesus Christ paid for *all* of our sins on the cross and that they are *all* paid for, the implications are enormous. We can go off-duty. We can step off the religious treadmill. We can go off the performance plan. We can reject the accusations of the enemy. We can feel safe and secure in God's love. Forever.

Let me give some of the biblical evidence for these strong statements about the cross.

*Christ came to die on the cross.* In Mark 10:45 Jesus proclaims, "For even the Son of Man came not to be served but to serve, and to give his life as a ransom for many." The central purpose of Jesus coming to earth was to die for our sins. Or, in Luke 19:10, Jesus says, "For the Son of Man came to seek and to save the lost." Jesus came to seek and to save lost sinners like you and me. He saved us by dying in our place.

*The cross is the primary proof of the Father's love.* Romans 5:8 declares, "But God shows his love for us in that while we were still sinners, Christ died for us." Or, consider 1 John 4:10: "In this is love, not that we have loved God but that he loved us and sent his Son to be the propitiation for our sins."

In fact, so many passages in the New Testament that refer to the love of God then refer immediately to the cross. Consider Galatians 2:20: "I have been crucified with Christ. It is no longer I who live, but Christ who lives in me. And the life I now live in the flesh I live by faith in the Son of God, *who loved me and gave himself for me.*"

Or, take the verse we just read in 1 John 4:10: "In this is love, not that we have loved God but that *he loved us and sent his Son to be the propitiation for our sins.*" This happens repeatedly in the New Testament—when God mentions His love for us, He often refers in the same verse to the cross as the essential proof of that love.

*The entire Bible points to the cross.* The Old Testament looks forward to the cross, and the New Testament looks back to the cross. Indeed, the first subtle pointer to the shed blood of Christ happened right after the fall of man in Genesis 3. In Adam and Eve's shame and guilt, they tried to cover their nakedness with fig leaves, but that covering would not do. What did God do instead? He covered them with animal skins, meaning that animals were slain, blood was shed, and substitutes died. This event was the first subtle pointer to a future day when the Lamb of God would be slain, when His blood would be shed, when He would become our Substitute.

The rest of the Old Testament continues to point toward the cross, with other sacrifices such as the sacrifice of animals by Noah after the Flood, the almost-sacrifice of Isaac, and the actual sacrifice of the ram in Genesis 22. There is also the entire sacrificial system, with thousands upon thousands of animals slain over the centuries. None could pay for our sin, but each would point to the Lamb of God who one day would take away our sin.

And besides all of this, there are the innumerable references to Christ in the Psalms and in the Prophets, highlighted by the graphic picture of the cross in Psalm 22 and culminating in the glorious hymn to the cross of Christ in Isaiah 53. The entire Old Testament points to Christ.

For example, consider the dramatic and repeated pointers to Christ and His cross in the magnificent passage of Isaiah 53:4-6:

> Surely he has borne our griefs
> and carried our sorrows;
> yet we esteemed him stricken,
> smitten by God, and afflicted.
> But he was pierced for our transgressions;
> he was crushed for our iniquities;
> upon him was the chastisement that brought us peace,
> and with his wounds we are healed.
> All we like sheep have gone astray;
> we have turned—every one—to his own way;
> and the Lord has laid on him
> the iniquity of us all.

If the cross of Christ is latent in the Old Testament, it is patent in the New Testament. For example, when John the Baptist first sees Jesus in John 1:29, he thinks of the cross:

"Behold, the Lamb of God, who takes away the sin of the world!" Each of the four Gospels focuses on the cross, with a disproportionate amount of each book describing the last week of Jesus' life leading to the cross. Jesus' testimony underscores the centrality of the cross in Mark 10:4: "For even the Son of Man came not to be served but to serve, and to give his life as a ransom for many."

There is also Jesus' grand statement from the cross: "It is finished!" (John 19:30), meaning that He had finished the work that the Father had sent Him to accomplish, the work of paying for sin.

And then there are the repeated references to the cross in Paul's writings and in other New Testament letters, especially in Romans and Hebrews but also throughout the New Testament. Revelation begins with that beautiful burst of praise to Christ:

> "To him who loves us and has freed us from our sins by his blood and made us a kingdom, priests to his God and Father, to him be glory and dominion forever and ever. Amen. Behold, he is coming with the clouds, and every eye will see him, even those who pierced him, and all tribes of the earth will wail on account of him. Even so. Amen" (Rev. 1:5b-7).

And when Revelation 5:9-14 gives us that glimpse of the worship of heaven for all eternity, it is no surprise that Jesus is praised as the Lamb of God who died for our sin.

And they sang a new song, saying,

> "Worthy are you to take the scroll
> and to open its seals,
> for you were slain, and by your blood you ransomed
>     people for God

from every tribe and language and people and nation,
and you have made them a kingdom and priests to our
   God,
and they shall reign on the earth."
Then I looked, and I heard around the throne and the
   living creatures and the elders the voice of many
   angels, numbering myriads of myriads and thousands
   of thousands, saying with a loud voice,
"Worthy is the Lamb who was slain,
to receive power and wealth and wisdom and might
and honor and glory and blessing!"
And I heard every creature in heaven and on earth and
   under the earth and in the sea, and all that is in them,
   saying,
"To him who sits on the throne and to the Lamb
be blessing and honor and glory and might forever and
   ever!"
And the four living creatures said, "Amen!" and the elders
fell down and worshiped.

What is my point in this chapter? From Genesis to
Revelation, there is a scarlet thread running through the Bible,
the shed blood of the Lord Jesus Christ for our sin. This is the
gospel! This is our story!

It is no surprise that Paul, the chief ambassador of the gospel
in the early church, the man who had once hated Jesus and now
loved Him fiercely, could proclaim, "For I decided to know
nothing among you except Jesus Christ and him crucified"
(1 Cor. 2:2).

Paul would also say in Galatians 6:14: "But far be it from me
to boast except in the cross of our Lord Jesus Christ, by which
the world has been crucified to me, and I to the world." This
was Paul's emphatic message—the cross, the cross, the cross!

And what happened on the cross? Sin was paid for. Your sin was paid for. *All* of your sins were paid for. They were nailed to the cross. Canceled. Eradicated. Forgiven.

This is the strong message of Colossians 2:13-14, which refers to the cross no less than five times:

> And you, who were dead in your trespasses and the uncircumcision of your flesh, God made alive together with him, having forgiven us all our trespasses, by canceling the record of debt that stood against us with its legal demands. This he set aside, nailing it to the cross.

Or there is the stunning statement of 2 Corinthians 5:21, that the Father made His Son to become sin so that we might become the righteousness of God:

> For our sake he made him to be sin who knew no sin, so that in him we might become the righteousness of God.

No wonder Paul could proclaim those unforgettable words of freedom and liberation in Romans 8:1: "There is therefore now no condemnation for those who are in Christ Jesus."

Friends, that's it. No condemnation, because our sin is paid for. *All* of our sin. *"It is finished!"*

When you sin, go to the cross. When you feel like a failure, go to the cross. When Satan accuses you (and he will), go to the cross. The cross, the cross, the cross!

We sing it with the old hymn, "What can take away my sin? Nothing but the blood of Jesus."

We also sing it in this hymn: "Jesus paid it all. All to Him I owe. Sin had left a crimson stain, He washed it white as snow."

What exactly did Jesus pay for when He paid it all? Sin. Your sin. *All* your sin.

Christian, *this* is the gospel: Christ died for sinners to set them free. If you have received the gift of the Savior, you are safe and secure forever and ever. What could you possibly do to lose that gift? All of your sin—past, present, and future—is already paid for.

The cross is the death knell to performance, to measuring up, to our efforts to earn our salvation. Religion says, *do* this. The gospel says, Christ has *done* this. Religion is spelled D-O, what I do. The gospel is spelled D-O-N-E, what Christ *has* done. Religion says, earn this. The gospel says, receive this. Religion says obey *in order* to be accepted by God. The gospel says obey *because* you have been accepted by God.

Friend, get off the Performance Plan. Get on the Grace Plan. Get on the Cross Plan. Get on the Blood of Jesus Plan.

Many of us have a deep-rooted drive to achieve, to work hard, to be the best. In school, I wanted to be the best student. I wanted to make all *A*'s. And then I got into sports and pushed my body relentlessly to achieve and excel and work. To perform.

My parents were not pushing me. *I* was pushing me. This was part of my brokenness, trying to prove I was a somebody.

And then I came to Christ and heard about grace. I knew that Christ had paid for my sin. Theologically, I knew it was all of grace. But somewhere deep in my soul, I still felt the need to work and earn and achieve. It was subtle and subconscious, but it was there—pushing, pushing, pushing, robbing me of joy and peace.

Dear one, face up to any residual performance mindset that you might have. Step off the religious treadmill. In Christ, you are free. "For freedom Christ has set us free; stand firm therefore, and do not submit again to a yoke of slavery" (Gal. 5:1). As Martin Luther King Jr. explained in another context, "Free at last! Free at last! Thank God Almighty! We are free at last!"

Brother, sister, it is vital in any struggle with OCD that we rest in the cross of Christ. Indeed, it is vital for all of us. Rest.

*Lord, this is our prayer, that we would see Christ in all His beauty and majesty, that we would see the cross in all of its power and finality, that we would see ourselves in all of our freedom and forgiveness. Lord, may we glory only in the cross of our Savior. Amen.*

# CHAPTER 12

# Do Not Battle Alone

The sixth tool: do not battle alone.

Throughout many years of my life, I battled OCD while telling hardly anyone because I was so embarrassed by my thoughts and fears: Was I really a Christian? Would I hurt someone I loved? Would I do something terrible? Would I cheat on a test in seminary? Was the Bible really true? What if I prayed to Satan instead of praying to God?

I did not know any other people who tormented themselves to the point of mental, emotional, and spiritual exhaustion. As I have already indicated, the person that I talked with the most about my struggles was Gayle. When we were dating, I knew that I had to be open with her, and I poured my heart out to her the best I could about what was going on. She listened carefully and patiently, responding with love and grace. Talking with her comforted me and assured me I was loved and accepted.

So, I would talk about my feelings at times with Gayle, especially when my thoughts got really bad. At times, I could not *not* talk about it because I would burst with pain if I held in my thoughts. But those times of transparency were the exception. For some reason, I mostly kept the problem inside, day after day, suffering in silence. I lived inside my own head. It was a lonely, painful struggle.

Occasionally, I would talk some with a friend if I felt he was safe and not easily shocked. I also began to mention it to our church from time to time, but these mentions tended to be brief and more about my past struggles than my current struggles. As I mentioned earlier in the book, I counseled with a few people, but only briefly—a couple of counselors during seminary, and one counselor after seminary. But I never told my parents about my struggles with OCD. I never talked with my close friend John Lodwick or other close friends about the problem. I hardly talked with anyone, mostly because I felt awkward and embarrassed—a lot of my struggles just felt weird. So, basically, I battled OCD alone. And this strategy did not work so well for me.

All of that changed in May 2011, at the age of 57, when the OCD spiraled out of control and I felt overwhelming fear and hopelessness. At that point, I had no choice. I *had* to talk about it. I *had* to get help. I was *desperate*.

That month, some close friends gave us the gift of a three-day vacation at Lake Travis outside of Austin, Texas. They wanted to bless us in some way and perhaps felt a little break would be good for us. So Gayle and I headed there for a brief vacation. My OCD had worsened over the last few months—I felt a lot of stress with church (probably more than I realized) that it made the OCD worse.

On the three-hour trip to Austin, I noticed that my OCD anguish seemed to be especially intense and after arriving in Austin the OCD did not leave but got worse. I would try to walk and pray in the neighborhood but was plagued and tormented by these horrible scrupulosity fears and thoughts. The pain was unrelenting. Every waking moment, my brain felt like it might explode or spin out of control. It seemed worse than ever.

After a day or so, I was in immense pain. I could not go on like this. My mental torment had never been this bad, and though I wanted to hide my struggle and battle it out alone, that was no longer an option. I was desperate, and I needed help. Finally, I broke down to Gayle, telling her I felt worse than ever and wasn't sure if I was going to make it.

Gayle immediately insisted that I call Peter Johnson, a young psychiatrist in our church who already knew about my struggles. Peter graciously took my call and told me he was putting me on Prozac. I was relieved—my anguish was so severe that I wanted to finally give medicine a serious try.

The next day, we left early from our trip because I was hurting so much. I needed to get back home and get help. On the way out of Austin we stopped at a Costco, and I waited in the parking lot for Gayle. Looking back, those 20 minutes in the parking lot were probably the worst 20 minutes of my life. I was afraid that the tormenting thoughts and fears would crush my brain, or that my brain would spin out of control and explode. My pain was so great that I even feared I would commit suicide at some point. I did not want to take my own life, but fear crept in that I might. I was so desperate. I tried to pray and to reason my way out of the tormenting thoughts, but I felt like I was drowning in quicksand and might not survive.

Would I ever get well? Would I survive this? Was there any hope?

When Gayle returned to the car and we began driving back to Houston, I told her how badly I was hurting. I was past hiding now. I was just trying to survive.

Besides the mental pain, I had this racing anxiety in my chest that would not go away. This was a new sensation and a scary one. It even felt a little difficult to breathe. I must have been experiencing a panic attack, which was new for me. And scary.

Gayle insisted that I again call Peter Johnson and tell him that I was worse. Could I begin the medicine immediately? Peter was incredibly helpful. "Yes, we can do that. But the medicine takes weeks to start making a difference." (I thought, *Oh, no! I cannot survive for weeks! I need help! Now*!) Fortunately, Peter told me he could also give me something for the anxiety in my chest, and that would help within 30 minutes. *(Oh, good! There is a ray of light!)*

We stopped by the pharmacy even before we went home. I began taking both medicines—Prozac for the OCD, Ativan for the anxiety. Peter was right. The anxiety began to dissipate after a half-hour, and I needed to take the Ativan for only a couple of days. *(Thank God that the anxiety lifted!)* But my ongoing mental torment was crushing. I was in survival mode.

I began to reach out to people in ways I never had. Part of me felt that our lead elder should know how much I was hurting due to mental pain—in fact, I felt I needed to tell several people what was happening to me. I asked our lead elder, Charlie Howell, if he and his wife Rhonda would meet with Gayle and me. Part of me felt that Charlie needed to know my mental fragility, but even more so, I needed Charlie and Rhonda's help. They were a godly, compassionate, praying couple.

Gayle and I met with Charlie and Rhonda for an hour or so. They listened. They cared. They accepted me. They did not seem shocked or horrified but prayed for me and reminded me of vital truths from the Bible.

We would meet several more times. Charlie and Rhonda gave me hope, they gave me love, and they cared. Rhonda suggested that I meditate on Romans 8 all summer, a suggestion that I accepted and one that proved extremely helpful. They talked with me and prayed with me about potential root causes.

They challenged me on issues like religious performance and intellectual pride. They spoke the truth in love.

Gayle and I also met with some close friends, Craig and Sheila Charbonnet. Craig told me about some of his own weird thoughts. *(Oh, good, Craig has awful thoughts and he seems normal.)* Craig also pointed me to the cross. Even if I committed the worst of sins, I was covered by the blood of Christ. This is the gospel—not performance, but grace! Though I believed in grace and had preached grace for years, I so needed to hear these words. And I needed the love and acceptance of friends who knew about my struggles and still loved me.

I also began to meet with our kids to tell them what I was going through. Gayle and I sat down with our oldest daughter Sarah and her husband Mike to tell them how I had been feeling. I regularly ran with our second daughter, Callie, and during a run I explained to her the crisis that I was experiencing. John Paul was away at school, so I told him on the phone. I was relieved to tell them. They needed to know how badly I was struggling, and I needed them to pray. Each of them handled the news graciously—they cared greatly but were unshaken.

I told others—my parents, my assistant Glena Siebert, other staff team members, and a few friends. More and more, I was bringing the problem out of the darkness and into the light.

About ten days after the crisis occurred, I was due to preach in our church again. What would I say about this crisis? How much should I say? Would this disturb people? Would this be a hindrance to them in some way?

But authenticity demanded that I tell our church. I could not struggle as much as I was struggling and preach a normal message, pretending that nothing was wrong. I decided on honesty and transparency. It would simply be inauthentic, dishonest really, to be struggling as much as I was struggling and *not* tell them. That would be phony. Besides, for all of those who were struggling with mental pain, and indeed all of those who were struggling with any overwhelming problem, I wanted them to know that their pastor understood what it meant to be weak and desperate.

So I told our people what was going on with me. In the past, I had primarily mentioned my OCD in terms of *past* struggles. But now I talked of my *present* struggle. I told them that I was hurting, that I was desperate, that I was not sure I was going to survive this.

The response was overwhelming. Overwhelming love. Overwhelming acceptance. I vividly remember Jay Myers, who had once been on our staff team, getting up and walking across the auditorium to give me a big hug of acceptance and love. Others responded with similar love. No one chastised me or rejected me, and I never felt judged or condemned in any way. The love and intercession of WoodsEdge was incredibly life-giving—every pastor should have such a church!

Moreover—this was the biggest thing of all for me—I told WoodsEdge I had to have their prayers. Desperately! I *wanted* their prayers. I *needed* their prayers. I knew it would make a vital difference if I had tons of people praying for me, and it did—I could sense the prayer. I believe that the healing which I have received over the last four years is largely the result of the prayers of WoodsEdge people. And I am deeply, deeply grateful. In many ways, my road to healing began that Sunday morning at WoodsEdge Community Church with my telling our congregation of my deep struggles and with our congregation responding in love and fervent prayer.

No longer did I hide the problem or keep it mostly private. I began to talk freely about the issue whenever it seemed helpful, whether helpful to me or helpful to others. It was no longer a secret or private matter.

I began meeting weekly with Michael Mickan, who not

only understands OCD but is extremely bright, helpful, and compassionate. Michael was a gift from God. Later, I began meeting with Adam Cole for healing prayer. Both Michael and Adam have become my close friends. God used them both immensely in my life.

Here's the point of my story: It simply does not work to live inside your own head. It does not work to walk alone and retreat into a cave of secrecy and isolation. God did not make us to live this way! God made us to live in community— genuine community. God Himself, our triune God, has always lived in community, and He made us in His image as relational beings. We thrive in community, and we wither in isolation.

We need each other. We need love. We need encouragement. We need intercession. We need people to share our burdens. We need people to weep with us and to rejoice with us.

So often, the American way is the way of privacy, the way of individualism. But this is not God's way. God's way is the way of community, the way of authenticity, the way of love. As C.S. Lewis has taught us, "the basic laboratory for knowing God is the Christian community."[1]

I am astounded by the example of Jesus at the Garden of Gethsemane in Matthew 26. This was the night before the crucifixion, and the thought of being separated from the Father and bearing the world's sin was nearly overwhelming to Jesus. He was struggling fiercely. *But He was not struggling alone.*

He called His disciples to Him, telling them that He needed them and needed their prayers. He was honest with them: "My soul is overwhelmed with sorrow to the point of death!" In other words, "I am hurting so badly that I feel like dying!"

Now, this is amazing. It would be one thing for me, a flawed, frail human, to be vulnerable and transparent about my struggle as Jesus was. No big deal. Yet, Jesus, the eternal Son of God, sinless and perfect, told the disciples that He was overwhelmed with sorrow, that He felt like dying, and that He needed them desperately! Such honesty! Such humility! Such bravery!

When this passage soaked into my soul, I realized that I could no longer be a pretender and at the same time be a follower of Jesus. I could no longer pretend that I was more spiritual than I was or that I had fewer problems than I did. I'm not as honest as I could be, but I'm no longer the poser that I once was. For the follower of Jesus, the life of constant posing and pretending is no longer an option.

Dear friend, Jesus sets the pace for authenticity. Be real. Be honest. Live in community. Share one another's burdens.

If you struggle with OCD, talk freely with your spouse or a close friend. Find a pastor or Christian counselor who understands the basics of OCD and who cares. Ask God for some intercessors who will battle with you. Find out if there is an OCD support group in your church, or at least someone who has struggled with OCD and will walk with you, sharing this burden. Talk with a trusted, highly-recommended psychiatrist, who can counsel you about whether you should take medicine.

If you cannot find a support group or mature believers who understand OCD, then at least get into a small group of caring believers. Be open about your struggles. They may not understand OCD, but they can love you and they can pray for you. And that is what you most need—their love and their prayers.

Dear one, whatever you do, do not walk alone.

*Lord, please help us to be real and honest. Help us to know we need people. Bring people into our life who can walk with us to wholeness and freedom. Amen.*

# CHAPTER 13

# Surrender

The seventh tool is surrender. Yes, the battle to overcome OCD is a *battle*. But, ironically, at the heart of winning this battle is surrender to Jesus, a deep and complete surrender of this entire quagmire of mental anguish.

Most of us who struggle with OCD have a tendency to be control freaks. We tend to want to control things around us and even within us, and we require things to be "just so," preferably perfect. But part of overcoming OCD is to surrender our need to be in control of *anything*.

Not long after my crisis occurred, I would begin having lunch with Michael Mickan (whom I mentioned earlier). Michael has been a gift of God, and it is impossible to overstate the role that he has played in my healing. During our lunches, he suggested something that would become an essential lesson for me: my ultimate problem was control. "Just as an alcoholic is powerless over alcohol and needs to admit it, so you are powerless over your need to control, and you need to admit it. You need to surrender this problem to God." He was not talking about a light and superficial surrender, but a deep and profound surrender. He was talking about such a deep surrender that if God wanted me to continue to struggle with OCD, that would be okay. "The main thing is not to get well, but to surrender this to God."

Frankly, that thought terrified me. I wanted to get well as much as a person trapped under water wants to breathe air. I fervently wanted the torment to go away. Yet, I sensed that Michael was right. At some deep level I did have a need to be in control. I needed to control these horrible thoughts so that they did not enter my brain, so that I could be "perfect"— uncontaminated by awful thoughts. However, my true need was not more control over my tormenting thoughts, but a profound and complete surrender to God.

Michael was an incredible blessingfrom God. He cared enough to walk with me in the battle, and he understood the OCD, giving me incredible insight. We began to meet weekly, and in the early months when I was still desperate, those weekly meetings were a lifeline for a drowning man. Michael was honest. Humble. Wise. He tended to ask me questions rather than give me simple answers, and pointed me to God, not himself, as the only one who could rescue me. At one our meetings, he also asked me to take medicine for a year without considering getting off the medicine, even as I got better. I agreed.

We began walking through the Alcoholics Anonymous (AA) 12-Step Program, with the approach that my basic problem was control. The first step of the 12-step program is to admit that you are powerless over your addiction. For those of us who battle OCD, we could say that our addiction is control. We are attempting to control things through our thoughts and actions, but control does not work for us. We must surrender all control to God, admitting that we are powerless to overcome our obsessions, our compulsions, and our need for control. We are powerless over our addiction.

Michael began to probe into root issues that may have led me to use hyper-control to anesthetize my pain. He also urged me not to fight so hard against the problem. "It's like you're caught in a bear trap, and every time you fight against the trap you make the problem worse. Stop focusing on the bear trap and start focusing on the Lord. Let Him release you from it." He encouraged me to stop using mental gymnastics to defeat a horrible thought or fear. "That's not working. You don't need to reason your way out of this quicksand. You need to surrender the problem to God."

Michael also recommended that I do more listening prayer—sitting silently before God and letting Him whisper to my soul. He told me that this act of surrender, this act of submission, was not only pleasing to God but was especially good for a control freak like me. "Why don't you stop doing all the talking and be quiet and listen during some of your prayer time?" I began doing that—though it was not easy to stop talking and still my mind. It is still not easy for me, but I have gradually been learning to calm the noise in my mind and listen, a practice that continues to help me let God take control of my thoughts.

My meetings with Michael gave me much more clarity about how I was using control in my life. The control is more subtle than obvious, more covert than overt. I may not be trying to control everything and everyone around me (though I do some of that), but inside I want to control thoughts and behavior with my religious performance or my mental gymnastics.

Ultimately, however, I am in control of nothing. I am a completely dependent creature—God alone is in control; God alone is sovereign. Seeking control is a futile attempt to play

God. Instead, I have to recognize that God alone is God. And I must surrender—totally, deeply surrender—to a sovereign God. "Lord, I surrender this completely to You. Whatever You want. Lord, I pray that You would remove it from me. Not my will, but Your will be done."

God's call to us in Psalm 46:10 is essentially a call to surrender: "Be still and know that I am God."

David also prays in Psalm 131,
   O Lord, my heart is not lifted up;
my eyes are not raised too high;
   I do not occupy myself with things
too great and too marvelous for me.
   But I have calmed and quieted my soul,
like a weaned child with its mother;
   like a weaned child is my soul within me.
O Israel, hope in the Lord
   from this time forth and forevermore.

Like David, we are in control of nothing. We do not lift up our heart, and we do not occupy ourselves with things too marvelous for us. We recognize we are like a weaned child in his mother's lap, completely dependent on God. That's you. And that's me.

Consciously, deliberately, deeply, surrender the OCD struggles to God.

*Oh, Lord, I surrender control. Whatever You want. Whatever, whenever, wherever, however. Without Your rescuing me, I am sunk. All, all, to Jesus I surrender. Amen.*

# CHAPTER 14

# Commit to Prayer

The eighth tool is prayer. Prayer is the sure indicator that we are trusting God and not ourselves. If we seldom pray, we are seldom trusting God. If we pray often, we are trusting God often. Prayer is the sign that we are depending upon God's grace, not our grit.

Prayer is not a preliminary endeavor before we get to the real work. Prayer *is* the real work. Prayer is the greater work. Prayer is the main work.

About two years after my crisis with OCD, God would give me another gift to help me on my journey. This gift was Adam Cole, an acquaintance at the time but a man who has since become my close friend.

Adam and Jennifer Cole were the founders and co-CEOs of a healthcare company, a quite successful business. But their marriage ran into difficult problems, and they were headed toward an ugly divorce, despite lots of input and counseling. I am an optimist and was praying regularly for them, but their problems seemed overwhelming even to me.

One day, a woman who worked for their company asked Jennifer to come to the woman's church for a special prayer session. The prayer session involved healing prayer, or inner healing, a time of asking God questions and then listening quietly to hear from God. Jennifer received incredible healing and freedom from this extended prayer time. She asked Adam if he would go meet with the pastor of that church, Chuck Miles, for healing prayer. Adam did go and had a similar breakthrough. Within a few weeks, their marriage had been completely transformed. It had gone from the cusp of a nasty divorce to a marriage characterized by forgiveness, healing, and love. I had never seen anything quite like it.

All of this happened a few years ago. Adam and Jennifer would work toward a wonderful, thriving marriage centered in Christ and would begin to help countless others receive freedom and wholeness through healing prayer. In fact, Adam now spends half of his work week running their company and the other half meeting with people for prayer.

I am one of those people that Adam regularly meets with.

I knew that Adam and Jennifer were meeting with others and helping so many people. When I heard that a young man with OCD, a young man that I knew, had received healing and freedom after praying with Adam, I thought, "I need to call Adam and get him to pray with me. I need more healing."

So Adam and I began meeting for prayer. We would ask God to reveal things to me—unconfessed sin, unforgiveness or anger toward someone, lies that I was believing about God or about myself. In response to these questions, the Lord would often put a word, a thought, an impression, or an image on my heart.

Over the last couple of years, Adam and I have met many times for prayer, and God has used these prayer times to bring healing and freedom. For example, God has set me free from seeing myself as an OCD addict, someone who *has* to struggle with OCD fears and torments. Instead, I see myself in essence as a much-loved child of God who was designed to walk in freedom and joy.

Also, God has freed me from the performance mindset, the thinking that I have to work hard and make sure that I do not mess up in order to earn God's approval. I do not have to live in the fear that I might "mess up" or "sin horribly." For this breakthrough, God again used the image from *The Shawshank Redemption*, showing me how so many of the prisoners could not live outside the prison walls. They were institutionalized.

I had to admit that there was a part of me that felt I *had* lived in the prison cell of OCD for 40 years, and the ruts in my mind ran deeply. Though I wanted to be free, part of me was afraid to live outside the prison walls, without the familiar cell of OCD, even though that cell could be so painful. I was a bit like Morgan Freeman's character, Red Redding, who was not sure that he could live on the outside as a free man. By contrast, Tim Robbins' character, Andy Dufresne, knew he could live on the outside, on a beautiful beach in Mexico. And he could hardly wait to get there.

I felt that God wanted me to realize that I too was a free man and could live outside the prison cell. It was a lie that I was institutionalized and had to struggle with OCD. In fact, I was not an OCD addict at all—I was a free man. As God tells us in Galatians 5:1, "For freedom Christ has set us free; stand firm therefore, and do not submit again to a yoke of slavery."

There is much that I could say to describe these times of healing prayer with Adam, and I could give many more examples. These prayer times have focused on Christ's love and His finished work on the cross. I have rejected lies that said I had to perform in order to earn God's favor, that the cross was not complete, that I had to submit to fear, that I needed to medicate my pain with self-punishment and other lies. And I more deeply received the truth that I was so loved by the Father, that I was safe forever and not on probation, that Christ had given me freedom from fear and performance.

It is difficult to express all that has been involved in these times of healing prayer and how God has used them. But I am deeply grateful that God brought Adam into my life to lead me.

To paraphrase Peter Johnson, my psychiatrist friend that I mentioned earlier,

> If you rely on therapy, you will get what therapy can do. If you rely on talking, you will get what talking can do. If you rely on medicine, you will get what medicine can do. And God might use these things. But when you rely on prayer, you get what *God* can do.

If you depend upon God in this battle, you will recognize that you cannot solve this problem on your own. You know that you need God, so you cry out to God. *You pray!*

Throughout the Bible, we see that God's people are people of prayer. In fact, prayer is at the heart of who we are as the people of God. God is a prayer-hearing God, and the people of God are a people of prayer.

So pray. Pray fervently. Pray with all your heart. Pray and do not stop praying. This is the point of Jesus' strong parable in Luke 18:1-8 about the persistent widow: we are to pray and not give up praying.

Furthermore, get others to pray for you. This is what Paul did: he was continually asking people to pray for him. In fact, in Romans 15:30 he asked the Christians at Rome to *strive* together in their prayers for him. He did not want wimpy prayers, but fervent, whole-hearted prayers—"I appeal to you, brothers, by our Lord Jesus Christ and by the love of the Spirit, to *strive* together with me in your prayers to God on my behalf."

Also, get others to not only pray *for* you but get them to pray *over* you and *with* you. Ask the elders of your church to pray for you, as James 5:14 commands us to do: "Is anyone among you sick? Let him call for the elders of the church, and let them pray over him, anointing him with oil in the name of the Lord."

You might even recruit a prayer team of trusted family and friends and ask them if they would intercede daily for your healing and wholeness. Ask them to go to battle for you, like a modern-day Epaphras. Paul writes of Epaphras, one of his co-laborers in Colossians 4:12-13: "Epaphras, who is one of you, a servant of Christ Jesus, greets you, always *struggling* on your behalf in his prayers, that you may stand mature and fully assured in all the will of God. For I bear him witness that he has *worked hard* for you and for those in Laodicea and in Hierapolis." I love having a prayer team of 70 or 80 people who regularly work hard in prayer for Gayle and me.

Why is prayer such a vital tool in this battle against mental anguish? Because you cannot solve this problem yourself. You need God's power, God's wisdom, God's protection, God's rescue. You need *God*.

You pray because you are depending upon God, not yourself. You pray because prayer is the real work, the important work. You pray because prayer accesses the omnipotence of God, unleashes the power of God, and because God is a prayer-hearing God. You pray because the Bible tells us—over and over again—to pray.

For example, Jesus tells us,

Ask, and it will be given to you; seek, and you will find; knock, and it will be opened to you. For everyone who asks receives, and the one who seeks finds, and to the one who knocks it will be opened. Or which one of you, if his son asks him for bread, will give him a stone? Or if he asks for a fish, will give him a serpent? If you then, who are evil, know how to give good gifts to your children, how much more will your Father who is in heaven give good things to those who ask him! (Matt. 7:7-11)

This does not mean that God gives us everything we want, when we want it, as if He is a genie in a bottle at our beck and call. No, He is the sovereign God and He gives us what is best for us. But He also tells us, repeatedly and emphatically, to pray. And so we pray. Indeed, we fill all heaven with our prayers.

And when we are praying, we find God. We meet God. We draw near to God. And that is the best thing of all.

So pray. Pray and do not stop praying. Pray and get others to pray. Pray because God tells you to pray.

*Lord, teach us to pray. Show us that You are a prayer-hearing God. Pour out a spirit of prayer upon us. Amen.*

# BENEFITS OF OCD

# CHAPTER 15

# What I've Learned from OCD

When my OCD reached a nadir in May 2011, I had been preaching through the Book of Romans for the previous nine months. I had made it through Romans 7, and my plan was to take a break from preaching Romans during the summer and then start back in the fall of 2011 with Romans 8. This was God's providence, because it was so good for me to live and soak in Romans 8 that fall after the intense struggle with OCD at the beginning of the summer. This was not only the passage that I most needed to be preaching out of, but it was also the passage that Rhonda Howell suggested I should meditate on every day that summer.

Romans 8 is, perhaps, the greatest chapter in all the Bible. This great chapter, chock full of the love and grace of God in Jesus Christ, would be my companion all summer during my devotional times with God, and it would be my companion all fall for my preaching. For six months, I would marinate and meditate on this splendid section of Scripture, something I would recommend for all those who struggle with mental disease (and for everyone else!)

Sometime during my preaching that fall, I came to Romans 8:28: "And we know that for those who love God all things work together for good, for those who are called according to his purpose." This passage tells us that God will bring good out of all the pain and suffering in our lives. Specifically, it told me that God would take all of the torment and anguish of OCD and bring good out of it for me. This does not mean that OCD is a good thing, because it is a cruel and painful condition. But God will redeem it—He will bring good out of the struggle. I will be a better person, a more faithful follower of my Lord Jesus, because of my OCD struggles.

I would like to share some of the ways that God has used OCD in my life.

1. **Growth in Grace**

The first benefit is that the grace of God has become more real to me. Since I first trusted Christ as my Savior 43 years ago, I have believed that salvation was by grace alone. Since I became a pastor about 35 years ago, I have preached the grace of God. But because of my struggles with obsessive-compulsive disorder, grace has become more real, more vital, more personal for me than it ever would have without my OCD struggles. I have had to remind myself many times: no matter what happens, no matter what horrible sin I might commit, all of my sins are covered by the blood of Christ. Christ's blood is greater than any of my sins and all of my sins. My forgiveness rests on the cross alone.

I have clung to verses like these, which trumpet the grace of God:

> Psalm 103:12: "As far as the east is from the west, so far does he remove our transgressions from us."

Romans 8:1: "There is therefore now no condemnation for those who are in Christ Jesus."

Colossians 1:13-14: "He has delivered us from the domain of darkness and transferred us to the kingdom of his beloved Son, in whom we have redemption, the forgiveness of sins."

Colossians 2:13-14: "And you, who were dead in your trespasses and the uncircumcision of your flesh, God made alive together with him, having forgiven us all our trespasses, by canceling the record of debt that stood against us with its legal demands. This he set aside, nailing it to the cross."

Galatians 5:1: "For freedom Christ has set us free; stand firm therefore, and do not submit again to a yoke of slavery."

1 John 4:10: "And this is love, not that we have loved God but that he loved us and sent his Son to be the propitiation for our sins."

I have grown to love the lines of the hymn "Nothing but the Blood": "What can wash away my sin? Nothing but the blood of Jesus." At a deep, personal, visceral level, I have learned to cling to grace. Like David, a murderer, like Paul, a murderer, I have become a lover of grace, a champion of grace, a trophy of grace.

## 2.   Rescue From Performance

This second benefit is similar to the first one, but a bit different. In the last few years since May of 2011, I have realized how much religious performance is in me, how much of the "earn this" mindset I have, how much of the "perform and measure up" mentality plagues me.

I know, intellectually, that I do not have to earn God's love and acceptance, and indeed *cannot* earn God's love and acceptance. Yet, deep inside, this performance mentality keeps rearing its ugly head. It is like a stubborn weed that keeps coming back.

I imagine that this struggle with performance is common, to some degree, to every Christ-follower because of our extensive human self-reliance, our proud self-exaltation, and our slowness to believe in God's grace. But if this struggle is common to all Christians, I seem to have a particularly strong case of it. Throughout the first 12 years of my schooling, I felt like I had to make the best grades in the class. Perhaps it is because I was a serious athlete for decades and it is deeply ingrained in me to work hard and achieve. The performance mindset runs so deeply in me. But that is no excuse!

More and more I am learning, with my heart and not just with my head, that performance has no place in the spiritual life. It is all grace. God's love is unconditional—not dependent on my performance but simply on His love—His unchanging love. He will never love me one bit less than He does right now, and He will never love me one bit more than He does right now. No matter my performance, His love is perfect, infinite, and unconditional.

3. **Dependence Upon God**

A third benefit of my mental struggles is dependence upon God. I feel more dependent on God for His strength and His power, more desperate for Him.

When you are overwhelmed with pain, when you are not sure that you are even going to survive, when you wonder if you will end up in a mental asylum, when every waking moment is clouded with dread and fear—at those times, you cannot help but realize your desperate dependence upon God. You cannot help but cry out to God for mercy.

Jesus begins the Beatitudes, and the entire Sermon on the Mount, with the words, "Blessed are the poor in spirit, for theirs is the kingdom of heaven" (Matt. 5:3). "Poor in spirit" means dependence upon God, desperateness for God, spiritual bankruptcy before God. God loves this poverty of spirit in us.

Dependence upon God is the same as faith in God, and all through the Bible we see how much that faith pleases God. In fact, Hebrews 11:6 tells us, "And without faith it is impossible to please him, for whoever would draw near to God must believe that he exists and that he rewards those who seek him."

Mental disease can be so painful. But it is fertile soil to learn absolute dependence upon the Lord.

4. **Humility**

Despite all the mental pain that I have experienced over the last 40 years, I still struggle with ego and pride—

way too much. How much worse this problem would be without these mental struggles! My pride would be out of control!

God has been so good to me. I am married to a beautiful and vivacious wife, Gayle, and we are closer now than we have ever been. We have three grown children who love Jesus with all their hearts, and each one is married to a spouse who loves Jesus just as much. We have grandchildren who are precious beyond words. Moreover, God allows me the privilege of pastoring an incredible church family, WoodsEdge Community Church, a church that is healthy and thriving. In my younger years God gave me the privilege of running marathons and other races around the world, including a second place in the 1978 Boston Marathon, and for a time I was the official American record-holder of the marathon (2:10:20, tied with Anthony Sandoval). In so many ways, God has been exceedingly gracious to me.

But the continual battle with mental anguish has kept me humble. Or, at least the struggle has kept me more humble than I would be without it. If it were not for years and decades of mental turmoil, perhaps I would be an egomaniac.

But with all that I have gone through, I feel no condescension toward anyone who has known failure, brokenness, and weakness, because I have known so much failure, brokenness, and weakness of my own. Recently, I spoke to 200 inmates at the Navasota prison. I told them my story about the grace of God in my life, including my journey with mental disease.

I also told them, and feel it deeply, that I had zero condescension toward them that they were in prison and I was not.

I do not identify with the Pharisee in Luke 18: "God, I thank you that I am not like other men, extortioners, unjust, adulterers, or even like this tax collector. I fast twice a week; I give tithes of all that I get" (Luke 18:11b-12). But I do identify with the tax collector: "But the tax collector, standing far off, would not even lift up his eyes to heaven, but beat his breast, saying 'God, be merciful to me, a sinner!'" (verse 13). Because of my battles with mental pain, I better understand his heart: "God, be merciful to me, a sinner!"

At one of my lowest points, Glena Siebert, my wonderful assistant at WoodsEdge, taught me a superb and succinct prayer: "Lord Jesus, Son of God, have mercy on me." Over and over that can be prayed, "Lord Jesus, Son of God, have mercy on me."

5.  **Time Alone With God**

Because of my mental struggles, I have a greater yearning to meet with God in an unhurried time of Bible reading, prayer, and worship. I take time to meet with God because I *want* to know Him better and love Him more. But I also *need* to meet with Him for my mental and spiritual sanity. I could not survive without this daily time alone with the Lord.

I feel the pulse of David's passionate prayer in Psalm 63:1:

O God, you are my God; *earnestly* I seek you;
my soul *thirsts* for you;
my flesh *faints* for you,
as in a dry and weary land where there is no water.

I resonate with Jesus' invitation in Matthew 11:28: "Come to me, all who labor and are heavy laden, and I will give you rest." I have learned that every day I need to come to Jesus, give Him my burdens and weariness, and receive His rest.

Because of my struggles with obsessive-compulsive disorder over the years, I am more desperate to meet alone with God every day. I hunger and thirst for Him in ways that would not have happened apart from the school of suffering.

Moreover, this daily time with God is richer than it would have been. It is not simply a matter of discipline— it is a matter of desperateness and urgency. I need this time alone with Papa.

6. **Closer Marriage**

My struggle with mental disease has made our marriage stronger. To be fair, my struggle with OCD has also hurt our marriage because so many times I have been preoccupied and aloof. Way too many times! On the other hand, this battle with mental disease has made me realize how much I need Gayle. It has helped me to be more vulnerable and open with her. I have realized even more how much I need her. Without this struggle, I am afraid that I would be far too independent and private, which are my natural tendencies and which do not make for an intimate marriage. But with mental pain, that independent streak in me has been dealt a death blow.

I am so grateful to Gayle for the way she has accepted me and supported me in the battle. I love her more because of it. And I know that she feels closer to me because we have walked this arduous road together.

7. **Listening Prayer**

Even if I had never had any mental struggles, I would still believe in listening prayer, but I do not think that I would realize so keenly how important it is. It is difficult to read the Bible, taking it at face value, and not believe that God speaks to us in all sorts of ways. Like David in the Old Testament, we need to be inquiring of God for direction and guidance. Psalm 46:10 tells us we need to be still before our God instead of incessantly talking and never listening. Because of my mental struggles, God gave me a deeper awareness of surrender to God, and part of surrender is quietness and listening to our King. The servant does not do all the talking!

Honesty compels me to clarify: I am not great at this. It is a struggle to quiet my mind, much less my mouth. I would rather talk than listen. But I am farther along in the journey than I would have been without the OCD struggles.

8. **Need for People**

Even without my mental struggles, I would still believe that we need community, that we need the body of

Christ, that we need each other. However, because of the pain I have experienced, I have felt this need for people and experienced it much more strongly than I would have without the suffering.

During the hardest times of my struggle, I *needed* Gayle. I *needed* my kids. I *needed* Charlie and Rhonda Howell. I *needed* Michael Mickan. I *needed* Peter Johnson. I *needed* the WoodsEdge family.

And God used people to help me. During the toughest period of my crisis, I reached out to a fellow pastor in the area, Ken Werlein, who has also struggled with OCD. Ken's hilarious and self-deprecating reply brought humor and help to the dead-serious issue and helped me fight the fight. If Ken could struggle so much and still lead a large church so effectively, maybe there was hope for me. (With Ken's permission, I have included his reply in Appendix 4.)

Again, the Bible is clear on the subject of community: we need each other. No man is an island, as John Donne put it centuries ago. We need authentic community. Yes, the Bible is clear, but it was the struggle with mental disease that moved this truth from my head to my heart. My need for people, my need for the body of Christ, became more obvious and urgent.

9. **Empathy**

A ninth benefit: I have deeper compassion for people with OCD because of my own struggles. I *hurt* for them. I *know* how painful it can be.

I also have more empathy for people with other mental diseases and for people who are hurting for any reason at all. Without the struggles I have been through, I just do not think that I would have had that much empathy for people in pain. But when you have suffered greatly, it is difficult *not* to empathize with others who suffer. Your own pain often can awaken compassion for others in pain.

## 10. Preaching

A tenth benefit of my mental struggles: my preaching has been deepened and enriched. Because of my struggles with OCD, my preaching ministry has more heart, more depth, more humility, more compassion, more vulnerability, more weakness, and more dependence upon God.

Both the school of suffering and the school of theology can be valuable, but the school of suffering can be invaluable. I am a stronger preacher because of the refining fires of suffering.

## 11. Helping People With OCD

An eleventh benefit: I have been able to help others who battle OCD. In my preaching, I openly talk about my struggles, and people in our congregation who struggle themselves, or who have family members who struggle, often email me or approach me after services. I email people articles and resources. I talk with people. For a time, I led a support group for fellow strugglers with OCD.

In 2 Corinthians, Paul gives voice to the concept that God comforts us in our sufferings so that we can comfort others who suffer: "Blessed be the God and Father of our Lord Jesus Christ, the Father of mercies and God of all comfort, who comforts us in all our affliction, so that we may be able to comfort those who are in any affliction, with the comfort with which we ourselves are comforted by God. For as we share abundantly in Christ's sufferings, so through Christ we share abundantly in comfort too" (2 Cor. 1:3-5).

## 12. **Greater Authenticity**

Because I talk openly about my weaknesses and struggles, especially my mental struggles, our church has become a safer place. The people of WoodsEdge know that church is not a place for perfect people, but a place for flawed people, broken people, hurting people. There is a widespread recognition at WoodsEdge that no one at our church has life together. No one is without pain and problems. No one has to put on a plastic smile and be a poser. Church is a safe place for hurting people.

Jesus loves this kind of authenticity. On the night before He was crucified, Jesus was suffering greatly because of the cross that He would face the next morning. His agony was not so much because of the looming physical pain, though that would be excruciating, but because of the looming spiritual pain of bearing the world's sin and being separated from his Father. Jesus was hurting and was unashamed to express this pain to His friends. He appealed to them with urgency: "Pray for me! Please pray for me!" At one point, He even says: "My soul is overwhelmed with sorrow, to the point of death" (Matt. 26:38 NASB) Jesus was essentially saying, "I am hurting so badly, I am in so much pain, that I feel like dying!"

This is incredible authenticity. Jesus set the bar of authenticity so high! When a pastor suffers so much from mental disease that he is not sure he will survive, authenticity comes easier. I do not imply that I am completely authentic or that our church is completely authentic. Of course not—not by a long shot. But at least I am more authentic than I would have been without the furnace of pain, and this has helped WoodsEdge become a more authentic community.

# CHAPTER 16

# Summary of Benefits

Every single one of these benefits has been valuable to me, and some of these have been absolutely crucial. These benefits are big. They are huge! And these are just the benefits that I have realized so far—I expect that over time I will discover even more. And who knows all that I will realize in eternity? To borrow C.S. Lewis's phrase, pain has "a severe mercy." The journey is severe, but there is mercy in it.

I would not want anyone to go through the pain I have experienced. But I also would not want to miss out on the things that God has done in my life through the pain. I hope I am done forever with the mental pain. I would love that! But I can give thanks to God for allowing me to struggle with OCD: "Father, I bless You for the pain of mental disease that I have experienced, as hard as it was, and I bless You for the good You have brought to my life through that pain."

Alan Redpath, a pastor and author from a previous generation, once wrote, "When God wants to do an impossible task, He takes an impossible man, and He crushes him." I do not know why it has to be so, but all through the Bible we see it: God uses suffering to shape His people.

Think of Job losing so much of his wealth and *ten* children. Think of Abraham and Sarah waiting 25 years to have the promised child, and the excruciating command to sacrifice Isaac. Joseph's brothers sold him into slavery and he was taken to a foreign land, where he was unjustly put into prison for 13 years despite his faithfulness.

Think of Moses, who spent 40 years in obscurity and then another 40 years with a difficult people in the desert. Ruth lost her husband, and David, whom Saul repeatedly tried to kill for no good reason, would later lose three children. Think of Jeremiah who was continually rejected as a prophet and who at one point was placed in a huge mud pit to die.

Think of Daniel, who was persecuted by jealous government administrators and even thrown into a lion's pit to be devoured. Mary knew that her own son would meet a gruesome end and would have to suffer through the crucifixion. Paul was beaten and stoned, jailed, and rejected over and over. Think of so many more people in the Bible and how much that each one learned in the furnace of pain. Suffering, more than anything else, is the best way for God to shape us.

The school of suffering is a hard school. But for the Christ-follower, the school benefits us, for our Lord will redeem the pain.

> "And we know that for those who love God all things work together for good, for those who are called according to his purpose" (Romans 8:28).

# APPENDICES

# APPENDIX 1

# Quick Suggestions

Here is a list of quick suggestions if you find yourself struggling with OCD.

1. **Call out to God.** He is a prayer-hearing God, and He is right there beside you. "Come to me, all who labor and are heavy laden, and I will give you rest" (Matt. 11:28).

2. **Meditate on Scripture.** Have a few key go-to verses.

   John 14:1. Do not let your hearts be troubled. Trust in God; trust also in me (NIV).

   Proverbs 3:5-6. Trust in the Lord with all your heart, and do not lean on your own understanding. In all your ways acknowledge him, and he will make straight your paths.

   Philippians 4:6-7. Do not be anxious about anything, but in everything by prayer and supplication with thanksgiving let your requests be made known to God. And the peace of God, which surpasses all understanding, will guard your hearts and your minds in Christ Jesus.

Galatians 5:1. For freedom Christ has set us free; stand firm therefore, and do not submit again to a yoke of slavery.

John 16:33. I have said these things to you, that in me you may have peace. In the world you will have tribulation. But take heart; I have overcome the world.

3. **Talk with a trusted friend.** Ideally, talk with someone who has been walking with you on this journey. Call a friend or get with a friend. Unburden your soul. Don't live inside your own head.

4. **Remind yourself that you are a much-loved, completely-forgiven, eternally-safe child of God.** Remind yourself that the blood of Christ covers all your sin. Remind yourself of who you are in Christ.

5. **Take this burden to the cross.** That is, tell Jesus you are bringing this burden or this fear to Him, and give it to Him. Recognize that, on the cross, Christ paid for all of your sins. Imagine giving this burden to Jesus on the cross.

6. **Surrender.** Do not strive. You are not trying hard to defeat this problem; rather, you are surrendering your burden to God. Surrender.

7. **Give thanks.** Start thanking God for all of the good things that He has given you. Maybe make

a list of all the things you are thankful for—put it in writing.

8. **Worship.** Sing to God a favorite song or hymn, perhaps over and over. Find a worship song on your iPad or iPhone. Worship.

9. **Remind yourself:** "This is not me. It is the OCD." This is at root simply a biochemical problem.

10. **Have someone pray over you.** Have a trusted friend pray for you, or perhaps have a group of people pray over you.

# APPENDIX 2

# Resources

Here are a few books and websites that you might find helpful.

1. The International OCD Foundation website:
   https://iocdf.org/

2. Obsessive-Compulsive Anonymous
   http://obsessivecompulsiveanonymous.org/

3. Here are a few websites specifically about scrupulosity:

   http://www.net-burst.net/guilty/scrupulosity.htm

   http://www.net-burst.net/guilty/OCD_treatment.htm

   http://www.net-burst.net/guilty/proof.htm

4.  Three books that are especially helpful:

    -   Bruce M. Hyman and Cherry Pedrick, *The OCD Workbook, 2nd Edition: Breaking Free from Obsessive-Compulsive Disorder* (Oakland, CA: New Harbinger Publications, 2005).

    -   Jeffrey Schwartz, *Brain Lock: Free Yourself from Obsessive-Compulsive Behavior* (New York: HarperCollins Publishers, 1996).

    -   Ian Osborn, *Can Christianity Cure Obsessive-Compulsive Disorder?* (Grand Rapids: Brazos Press, 2008).

5.  You might consider the book *Grace Abounding to the Chief of Sinners* by John Bunyan, in which he outlines his own struggles. Here is a website containing a free copy of Bunyan's book:

    www.gutenberg.org/cache/epub/654/pg654.txt

# APPENDIX 3

# Summary of Jeffrey Schwartz's 4-Step Treatment Plan

## What is Jeffrey Schwartz's recommended treatment?

Schwartz summarizes his approach to treatment: "'It's not me—It's my OCD.' That is our battle cry. It is a reminder that OCD thoughts and urges are not meaningful but that they are false messages from the brain. Self-directed behavior therapy lets you gain a deeper understanding of this truth."[1]

Schwartz also gives this four-step summary[2]:

Step 1: RELABEL
Recognize that the intrusive obsessive thoughts and urges are the RESULT OF OCD.

Step 2: REATTRIBUTE
Realize that the intensity and intrusiveness of the thought or urge is CAUSED BY OCD; it is probably related to a biochemical imbalance in the brain.

Step 3: REFOCUS
Work around the OCD thoughts by focusing your
attention on something else, at least for a few minutes.
DO ANOTHER BEHAVIOR.

Step 4: REVALUE
Do not take the OCD thought at face value. It is not
significant in itself.

# APPENDIX 4

# Ken Werlein

Ken Werlein is a close friend who pastors a large and wonderful church in Houston called Faithbridge. During my worst crisis with OCD, in May of 2011, I reached out to Ken. He emailed me back this transparent and hilarious note that greatly encouraged me.

Hi, Jeff-

I'm understanding you've hit a bump with your OCD. I've had it since childhood! Let's get together.

Anxiety disorder was added to my diagnosis in 2004 when Suzanne was pregnant with Wesley and I was working feverishly to raise the money for our phase 1 construction. I started having little tremors in my hands and teeth and couldn't stop it; thought I was dying of ALS or surely had Parkinson's. I also had daily anxiety attacks which felt like I was dropping off a cliff but never could hit bottom and be done with it. I was a wretched mess.

Doctor gave me Lexipro and that made all the difference, though it did plump me up a happy 20 extra pounds. So I weaned off about a year or so later.

Then in 2007, when Suzanne was pregnant with William, I started noticing I had some of the symptoms of colon cancer, until they did a colonoscopy and found my colon clean as could be. Several weeks later, I had chest pains and went to the hospital; stayed a day and night and went through all those tests, too.

How many pastor friends do you have who've survived ALS, Parkinson's, colon cancer, and heart attacks? ☺ (Sometimes I marvel at all the ailments I've managed [to] come through. ☺ )

About then Suzanne demanded, "Back on the meds, buddy!" So I went with Prozac that time, which did not plump me up any further, but definitely got my anxiety, hypochondria, and OCD back to a manageable baseline.

Add to all this the fact we Wesleyans aren't supposed to believe in eternal security—you can just imagine how many times I've been to hell and back. ☺

Glad to know we might have more in common than I even realized! But making fun of myself helps. Let's have lunch, maybe Thursday?

Praying for you, bro-

Ken

P.S. I can regale you with still more stories—like the one of many times Suzanne had to take to me to [the] E.R., but it really wasn't convenient for her that day, so she dropped me off at the E.R. curb and told me she'd be at the grocery store—but to call her when I was feeling better and she'd swing by and bring me home. ☺

Ken also wrote this little piece on his experience:

### My Experience with Anti-Depressant/Anxiety Medication

Ten years ago, my wife, Suzanne, was pregnant with our first child and I was working feverishly to raise 10 million dollars so our church could complete our first building project and move from rented school facilities into a permanent structure.

During that season, I began noticing little tremors in my hands. My teeth chattered, too, whenever I held them in a closed position. I went straight to the internet and started researching. Within hours I reached the grim conclusion that I must have Parkinson's disease or ALS. Either way, I concluded I was not long for this world.

I emailed all my prayer partners, requesting prayer support from family and friends, alike. I surrendered it all to the Lord over and over, confessed every known sin I'd ever committed, and I meditated constantly on passages like Philippians 4:6-8 and Matthew 6:31-34. But nothing changed. A minute after awakening each morning, my mind fixated on my symptoms. Throughout a normal day, I could not shake these perilous thoughts for longer than five minutes at a time.

After a week or two of this, I began searching out the best neurologists in Houston and working every connection I had to get an appointment, which I obtained surprisingly quickly. On the morning of that appointment, I drove to the medical center crying some, just thinking of how my family would not have me around much longer—or certainly not in my current strong condition.

Upon my arrival, I prayed once more in the parking lot, mustered courage, marched inside, rode the elevator up, and signed in at the doctor's office. Within minutes I had spoken with the neurologist, reported all my symptoms to her, and was ushered down the hall to begin a battery of testing. It took an entire morning, but I figured every hour they spent put me an hour closer to the truth I could no longer avoid.

Finally I returned to the examination room and awaited the neurologist's reappearance. She came in, sat down, shook her head, and looked sympathetically at me. She spoke softly but earnestly, and said, "Ken, you do *not* appear to have Parkinson's. Nor do you have ALS." I sat there stunned!

Befuddled, I asked, "Then why on earth am I shaking and rattling, and feeling like I am coming unglued!?"

She smiled and said, "Look, you're soon to be a first-time daddy, and you're leading a very large church through a sizable project. You're under a lot of stress, and I believe you are wrestling with something called anxiety. You need to go back to your family doctor and discuss an SSRI [selective serotonin reuptake inhibitors] form of medication (e.g. Prozac, Lexipro, Zoloft, etc.)"

"Good grief!" I sighed. Several weeks earlier my family doctor had made the same suggestion. But me? Taking the medication that depressed and anxiety-prone people take? "No way! I might be a little shaky, but I am no psycho," I thought to myself. After another week or so, I acquiesced, knowing deep down I could not keep going the way I had been.

Within a few weeks, I noticed something: I hadn't fixated on any bodily ailments or even thought of dying for days! Nor was I feeling so shaky anymore. I actually felt . . . like *me* again. I felt confident that I would surely live to see my newborn son, and likewise confident that the Lord would bless our church with the resources we needed for building a permanent home.

Better yet, my wife told me I was like my old self again and *tons* more fun to be with. My staff at church also commented about how much calmer the atmosphere of our entire office had become in the recent weeks.

On one hand, I was elated to feel like my old self again! On the other, though, I was a little embarrassed that medication appeared to be integral in this process.

A year or so later, I figured I'd had enough of the Lexipro, so I decided to wean off. I followed the plan carefully outlined by my doctor, which spread out over several weeks, so as not to shock my system. But I opted not to tell anyone else of this decision—and certainly not my wife. I figured she would be the ultimate litmus test.

Things went along reasonably well for a month or two. I definitely felt edgier; but I managed to hold most of it in. One night, though, as Suzanne and I were leaving a restaurant on our date night, our conversation grew very tense; downright argumentative! We hadn't had a fight like it in years.

Right in the middle of it all, as if struck by a lightning bolt, she blinked as if having an epiphany, and blurted out the mother of all dreaded questions: "Ken, have you been taking your medication?"

I was busted. Part of me wanted to lie, but I knew that would never work.

I confessed to having weaned off the medication several weeks earlier.

"Aha!" she exclaimed. "I knew something was feeling strangely different about you!"

She shook her head in apparent disgust and stared me down. Then her eyes lit up and she smiled. After that she started chuckling. I asked her to please keep things serious, but she could not. Her chuckle turned into outright laughter. After a minute of watching her laughing at me, I finally had to start laughing, too.

Suzanne reached across the front seat and grabbed my hand, pointed her other hand at me, gasped for a breath between her guffaws, and exclaimed, *"I am so glad we had this talk! So now, buddy, back on your meds!"*

Several weeks later, my edginess, irritability, anxiety, hypochondria, and OCD tendencies were down to a manageable baseline. It was then I had to acknowledge the truth about this type of medication: it really does help. At least it helps me.

Certainly I am no doctor, and I realize there are all sorts of categories of medication I could never converse about—

but I know something about SSRI's, and that having a little of one in my system helps me to do life much better, whether it is pastoring, praying, parenting, or partnering with my wife.

I have been honest and self-deprecating throughout these ten years, sharing all this publicly in several sermons, because I have realized three things:

1. I have learned there are a lot more people like me than I ever imagined. Men and women in my congregation consistently thank me when I recount this story in private, and sometimes even in sermons. People confide in me about how helpful my story was in normalizing their need for some help. Marriages are better, families are better, and even people's intimacy with the Lord is better as a result.

2. I have also learned that pastors and leaders are especially prone to the sorts of inner struggles I have described. I used to think it was solely spiritual warfare (1 Peter 5:8 sort of stuff); but having discussed all this with a number of folks, I have concluded there is often something else at play here. Specifically, most people who possess the competencies to lead a large organization also possess an innate ability to anticipate, intercept, and solve significant problems before the rest of the pack ever gets there. (That's why we leaders lie in bed thinking while the rest of the world sleeps!) Subsequently, many of us who possess a leadership gifting are often also strung a little too tightly for our own good (and for others' comfort). For another

confirming perspective regarding the depression side of the anxiety/depression conundrum, take a listen to well-known Pastor Tommy Nelson, at: http://www.dts.edu/media/play/a-christian-looks-at-depression-tom-nelson.

3. Finally, I have learned to *get over it* about my need to take medication. I have come to realize that, gratefully, we live in an era in which heart patients can receive precisely the medication they need. So can thyroid patients, and blood pressure patients, and diabetics. A hundred years ago I suppose it was not so, but now it is! James 1:17 tells us that "every good and perfect gift comes from above," and I consider SSRI medication a gift from above.

In the same way I would shamelessly tell a heart, thyroid, or diabetic patient (especially one with young children and many potential years of crucial life ahead), "Look, you have a moral obligation to take your medicine," I have come to realize I have the same obligation—just to make sure none of the wheels on my wagon start getting wobbly again.

Taking my anti-depressant/anti-anxiety medication is one of the ways I have learned to love the Lord with all of my heart, my soul, *and my mind*.

# APPENDIX 5

# Family Members

### Loving others who have OCD

What did God use to bring healing in my life? Certainly, there were the prayers of God's people, especially the people of WoodsEdge Church. God used Dr. Peter Johnson, both his counseling and the medicine he prescribed. He used Charlie and Rhonda Howell, Michael Mickan, and Adam Cole. He used the acceptance and love of the WoodsEdge Church family, which was so huge for me. And there were other people that God used in various ways and in varying degrees.

But behind all of this was Gayle. When we were dating, I told her as much as I could about my mental struggles. From that time to the present, she has responded in an incredible way, with compassion and acceptance. Not once has she belittled me, shamed me, or even hinted of rejecting me. For over 35 years, she has been unfailingly loving. She has prayed, cared, been patient, put up with my being preoccupied and distant, and, so often, she has endured more than any wife should have to endure.

When I was in the throes of my crisis in 2011, we had driven back from Austin and were sitting in the car at the drive-through pharmacy. While we were sitting there, Gayle said to me, "This is going to be good. God will bring good out of this." I was in so much pain that I could barely hear her. I felt like I was barely surviving. But in her words, there was hope, and I needed some bit of hope to cling to. Besides, she would be right.

It is not easy to be married to someone with OCD. For so long I was preoccupied with tormenting thoughts. Often, in earlier years, she felt that I must be angry with her, but I was actually fighting imaginary monsters in my own head. Plus, at times I was difficult and eccentric, both in my attitudes and in my actions. As it is said, too truly, "A perfectionist is one who takes great pains—and gives them to others!" This is true for the perfectionist, but it is especially true for someone with full-blown OCD.

Gayle's love, acceptance, and endurance have been incredible. She has been the most important person, by far, in my healing. When I needed courage to go talk with other people, she was there. "Yes, go talk to the Howells." "Good, you are going to meet with Michael again. Great!" "Yes, go pray with Adam Cole."

Gayle's personality is very different from mine. She has always been fun-loving. She enjoys putting whoopee cushions under people's chairs. She loves to laugh. She is the opposite of someone who is over-scrupulous, rigid, and perfectionistic. Her fun-loving and mischievous personality has been so good for me. I think if I would have married someone who was over-serious and perfectionistic, my OCD struggles would have been much worse. Sometimes, when I shared a fear or struggle with Gayle, she would empathize and care, but also she would let me know, often in a light-hearted way, that the fear was just ridiculous and I could let it go.

Gayle has been God's greatest gift to me in this bloody battle. What if you have a family member who struggles with OCD—perhaps a spouse, a child, a sibling, or a parent? What should you do?

First of all, you are doing it now—you are learning about OCD. You are seeking to better understand it. I encourage you to continue to learn more about OCD and mental disease. You do not have to become an expert (I am not an expert), but you need to understand the basics. Consider reading *The OCD Workbook* by Bruce M. Hyman and Cherry Pedrick, and also consider reading one or two other books and looking through a few websites, such as the website of the International OCD Foundation.

Let me caution you: you will never fully understand OCD unless you have the disorder yourself. But you do not need to understand it completely. It's not so important that you say to your family member, "I understand how you feel," because actually you don't. However, you can learn the basics and be able to say, "I care about what you're going through."

Second, and most importantly, you can pray. Prayer is the real work. Prayer is where the power is because prayer accesses the omnipotence of God. God loves it when we pray, and the most important thing we can do for any human being is to pray. Pray, keep praying, and do not lose heart. Luke 18:1 explains, "And he told them a parable to the effect that they ought always to pray and not lose heart." God loves it when we keep praying and do not lose heart, because praying always expresses faith in God, dependence upon God. You might not have perfect faith, but you have enough faith to pray. The most important thing you can do for your family members is to pray that God would pour out His healing grace upon them.

Next, be a great listener. Ask your family members how they are doing, how it is going, and if they have been struggling much lately. It shows that you care, that you are interested. This is especially critical for family members living inside their own heads and battling OCD alone. Seek to draw them out and get them talking.

In addition, recognize that your spouse, your child, or your family member did not choose to have OCD. Do not blame your family member for what is in essence a biochemical problem. Hyman and Pedrick offer this caution: "Realize that people with OCD cannot control the powerful urges they are experiencing . . . They do not *choose* to have OCD any more than a person chooses to have diabetes or thyroid disease."[3]

Fifth, be crystal clear that this problem is not your fault. As Hyman and Pedrick explain, "You did not cause the OCD. The causes of OCD are not related so much to the environment as they are to genetic and biological vulnerability. Stop feeling guilty—you did not cause the OCD. Guilt will only drain you of the energy you need to deal effectively with OCD."[4] Do not blame yourself, especially if you are a parent. Reject any false guilt, which simply is a tool of the enemy, who is known as "the accuser of our brothers" (Revelation 12:10). OCD is not your fault.

Also, recognize that you cannot fix this problem. You cannot rescue your family member because you are not God. You can help—you can encourage, pray, and support. But it is not up to you to fix this problem.

Next, encourage your family member to get help. Of course, if you are the parent of a child struggling with OCD, you can insist that your family member gets help. But even if the family member is an adult, you can encourage your loved one to see a doctor, a counselor, or a pastor. Talk to them about going to a support group, trying special prayer, or taking other steps to get help. Walk with them. Give them a sense that they are not alone. You are right there with them, battling alongside them.

Eighth, do not let anything they say shock or surprise you. Do not respond, "Oh, I can't believe that you said that!" If you respond with shocked repugnance, you can be sure they will stop talking with you about this problem. Hyman and Pedrick state, "Expect that OCD symptoms make no sense. They are inconsistent. Dr. Hyman once had a patient who was terrified of germs. He lived in constant horror of the possibility of anyone getting saliva on him. But he loved it when, upon arriving home from work, his dog joyously licked his face. That's the nature of OCD. All too often, it makes no sense."[5] Hyman and Pedrick also explain, "Realize the symptoms have little or no *symbolic meaning*. It is useless to interpret the symptoms as having any meaning beyond the impact they have. The symptoms mean nothing other than 'It is just OCD.'"

Additionally, do not label your family member with OCD. This is not who they are. They may struggle with this problem, but OCD is not their core identity, so do not see them as an OCD addict. See them as a precious child of God, much loved by Him.

Tenth, do not enable your family member in their OCD. For example, if they want to change their clothes six times a day, do not do their laundry. They can do their own laundry.

In addition, do not embarrass or ridicule your family member in front of others. That is simply not loving.

Last, encourage your loved one that there is hope. Never give up. Remind them that so many people get well. Give them hope. Hyman and Pedrick offer this helpful advice: "Use verbal praise to reward progress, no matter how small and seemingly inconsequential it is. Remember, reducing checking from fifty to forty checks may not seem like a big deal to you, but to the person with OCD, it can be a major step."[6] Hyman and Pedrick also caution, "Expect relapses and backsliding. Progress is often 'two steps forward and one step back.' Retrain the tendency to become discouraged and negative. Stay positive, keep working at it, and the OCD *will* get better!"[7]

*(Note: Hyman and Pedrick recommend the Self-Directed Program, which they outline in "The OCD Workbook." This is a form of cognitive behavior therapy. See Appendix 2 for more information about the book.)*

## Living with family when you have OCD

In *Brain Lock,* Schwartz advises how to successfully interact with family members if you suffer with OCD:

1.  OCD always involves the family.

2.  Be aware of how OCD symptoms affect your loved ones.

3.  Be aware of using OCD symptoms as a way of distancing yourself from the needs of your loved ones.

4.  Avoid at all costs using OCD symptoms as a way of demonstrating anger or annoyance at your loved ones.

5.  Help family members learn more about OCD and the Four Steps to help them avoid nonproductive criticism and facilitating your symptoms.

6.  Family members can make excellent co-therapists. Encourage them to help, not criticize.

7.  Mutual acceptance in the context of constructive interaction is very conducive to improved performance of the Four Steps.[8]

# APPENDIX 6

# Signs of OCD in Children

Hyman and Pedrick list the following signs of OCD in children:

- Being overly concerned with dirt and germs
- Frequent hand washing or grooming, often in a ritualistic manner; red, chapped hands from excessive washing
- Long and frequent trips to the bathroom
- Avoidance of playgrounds and messy art projects, especially stickiness
- Untied shoelaces, because they may be "contaminated"
- Avoidance of touching certain "unclean" things
- Excessive concern with bodily wastes or secretions
- Insistence on having things in a certain order
- Having to count or repeat things a certain number of times; having "safe" or "bad" numbers

- Repeating rituals, such as going in and out of doors a certain way, getting in and out of chairs a certain way, or touching certain things a fixed number of times. This behavior may be disguised as forgetfulness or boredom.

- Excessive checking of such things as doors, lights, locks, windows, and homework

- Taking excessive time to perform tasks. You may find a lot of eraser marks on schoolwork

- Going over and over letters and numbers with pencil or pen

- Excessive fear of harm to self or others, especially to parents

- Fear of doing wrong or having done wrong

- Excessive hoarding or collecting

- Staying home from school to complete assignments, checking work over and over

- Withdrawal from usual activities and friends

- Excessive anxiety and irritability if usual routines are interrupted

- Daydreaming (the child may be obsessing)

- Inattentiveness, inability to concentrate or focus (often mistaken for ADD)

- Getting easily, even violently, upset over minor, trivial issues

- Repetitive behaviors including aimlessly walking back and forth in the halls

- Unexplained absences from school

- Persistent lateness to school and for appointments
- Excessive, repetitive need for reassurance for not having done, thought, or said something objectionable
- Asking frequent questions, when the answer has already been given
- Rereading and rewriting, repetitively erasing[9]

# NOTES

## What Is OCD?

1. Bruce M. Hyman and Cherry Pedrick, *The OCD Workbook, 2nd Edition: Breaking Free from Obsessive-Compulsive Disorder* (Oakland, CA: New Harbinger Publications, 2005), 7.

2. Ibid., 7.

3. Ian Osborn, *Can Christianity Cure Obsessive-Compulsive Disorder?* (Grand Rapids: Brazos Press, 2008), 26-27.

4. Jeffrey Schwartz, *Brain Lock: Free Yourself from Obsessive-Compulsive Behavior* (New York: HarperCollins Publishers, 1996), xi-xii.

## How Common Is OCD?

1. Hyman and Pedrick, 15.

2. Osborn, 29-30.

## Types of OCD

1.  Hyman and Pedrick, 7-9.

## Examples of Obsessions and Compulsions

1.  Ibid., 18-23.

## Causes of OCD

1.  Schwartz, xxxi-xxxii.
2.  Ibid., 208.
3.  Hyman and Pedrick, 25-26.

## Common Faulty Beliefs

1.  Ibid., 98-100.

## Immerse Yourself in God's Love

1.  A.W. Tozer, *The Knowledge of the Holy* (New York: HarperOne, 1961), https://books.google.com/books?id=7qMko7zfcqIC&printsec=frontcover&source=gbs_ge_summary_r&cad=0#v=onepage&q=%22when%20we%20think%20about%20God%20is%20the%20most%20important%20thing%20about%22&f=false, 1.

2.  Tozer, *The Root of the Righteous: Tapping the Bedrock of True Spirituality* (Camp Hill, PA: WingSpread Publishers, 1986), https://books.google.com/books?id=uHMYAgAAQBAJ&printsec=frontcover&

source=gbs_ge_summary_r&cad=0#v=onepage
&q=god%20is%20easy%20to%20live%20with&f=
false.

3.  Ibid.

4.  Martin Luther, quoted in Roland H. Bainton, *Here I Stand: A Life of Martin Luther* (Nashville: Abingdon Press, 1978), https://books.google. com/books?id=NFbHwGvbIO0C&printsec=front cover&source=gbs_ge_summary_r&cad=0#v= onepage&q&f=false, 223.

5.  G. K. Chesterton, "The Scandal of Father Brown," *The Collected Works of G. K. Chesterton* (San Francisco: Ignatius Press, 2010), https://books. google.com/books?id=52eW6bDPq_wC&printsec =frontcover&source=gbs_ge_summary_r&cad= 0#v=onepage&q&f= false, 409.

## Do Not Battle Alone

1.  C. S. Lewis, quoted in Dr. Larry Crabb and Dr. Dan Allender, *Encouragement: The Unexpected Power of Building Others Up* (Grand Rapids: Zondervan, 2013) https://books.google.com/books?id=hKKOMH pW7O8C&pg=PT33&lpg=PT33&dq=The+basic+ laboratory+for+knowing+God+is+the+Christian +community&source=bl&ots=_QfgO4-nyr&sig=_ qaqCaT6TcW5z1-g6hK80XH6594&hl=en&sa=X &ved=0ahUKEwic_uvp6YTLAhUI6CYKHasBBe 4Q6AEIHTAA#v=onepage&q=The%20basic%20 laboratory%20for%20knowing%20God%20is%20 the%20Christian%20community&f=false.

## Appendices

1. Schwartz, *Brain Lock*, 208.
2. Ibid., 219.
3. Hyman and Pedrick, 49.
4. Ibid., 49-50.
5. Ibid., 50.
6. Ibid., 49.
7. Ibid., 49.
8. Schwartz, 181.
9. Hyman and Pedrick, 184-185.